"Jason was the first person that gave me a full-time coaching job, he also shepherded my journey from Albany CrossFit to where I am now and urged me to pursue my next steps, even though that meant leaving him and the gym. He leads from the front and by example. Listen to him, as he has good stuff to give!"

—Austin Malleolo

"In *Best Hour of Their Day* Jason has crafted a solid resource to help improve upon the impact a Coach has on clients."

—Chuck Carswell

"Jason absolutely crushed it with Best Hour of Their Day! Practical, actionable advice for getting the most from people that you can implement immediately. Not useful just for coaches, but for anyone that needs to excel at leading and engaging small groups."

—Chuck Bennington

"Jason Ackerman has a curious mind, humble spirit and genuine desire to share what he's learned along the way."

—Adrian Bozman

"Jason has been involved in numerous areas of the fitness industry and I count myself uniquely fortunate to have been a part of his journey. His longterm belief and practice of improving our lives and the lives of others through fitness unfolds into much more than bench presses and bro reps. Here we have a collection of lessons learned that will inspire us and those around us to become the best version of ourselves."

—JAMES HOBART

"If you want to learn about the history and development of CrossFit, Jason is your man. He's seen it all as a coach, affiliate owner, certification staff and everything in between. Great way to learn from one of the people who helped build this community."

—DAVID OSORIO

"Jason embodies both passion and professionalism. In my more than a decade of affiliate ownership and over six years of working on CrossFit seminar staff he is one of the people I respect and admire the most. The book is an example of what affiliate owners and coaches should be striving for in order to promote the health and wellbeing of their clients."

—JASON FERNANDEZ

BEST
HOUROF
THEIR
DAY

JASON ACKERMAN

Best Hour of Their Day

Editors: Andrea Cecil Topper, James McDermott
Cover photo: Nate Totten
Book cover design and formatting services: Victor Marcos

www.besthouroftheirday.com

Contents

Prologue

Hard to believe it's been over 25 years since I first stepped foot inside of a gym, I remember it like it was yesterday. The shiny equipment, the mirrors lining every wall, the rows and rows of cardio equipment, treadmills, ellipticals, recumbent bikes, oh my! At 13 years old I was young and impressionable, I was in awe of these men, throwing around weight like it was nothing, to me they were larger than life, it was a magical feeling. The excitement I would feel as my mom and I loaded into our Chevy Blazer and drove the 15 minutes down Route 6 to Club Fit was like a drug and I was addicted. So, like any addict would do, I did everything possible to ensure I could be there every day.

I learned many lessons in that gym and continued to learn along my fitness journey from wrestling, bodybuilding, yoga and CrossFit. The most important lesson I learned was this: Your "why" will guide you. It will carry you through tough times and help you overcome adversity.

Knowing and having a deep understanding of your "why" is the key to success. Without it, it's easy to quit, to give up, to become complacent, to live an ordinary life. Chances are that if you're reading this book, you want a life worth living.

It starts with your "why."

I had opened my third CrossFit affiliate when I thought I figured out my "why." I now realize it was with me all along, and it all started at the gym.

Since finding the gym—and later CrossFit—I have been able to meet thousands of people, travel the world, and maintain a lifestyle of health and fitness. It was by doing these things I learned the ultimate lesson, the value of real human connection. It's what helped me develop not only as a coach, but as a husband, son, friend, and enriched my sense of purpose in this world. I hope this book helps you do the same.

*

On paper, I'm a shitty trainer. I lack an exercise-science degree and my 5-foot-3 frame doesn't exactly look the part. I don't care much for science or math or anatomy. I'm not dumb. I did well in school making the dean's list most semesters in college and finished my master's degree with a summa cum laude GPA. But classroom stuff just isn't my strong suit. I learn by doing and have always had a passion for coaching. The only reason Joe, the manager at Club Fit in Peekskill, New York, finally hired me at 18 was because I kept asking to train people. I think he finally got tired of saying "no."

Shortly after starting that first personal-trainer job in 1996, I had a wait list of people who wanted me to train them. I loved watching Joe's quizzical expression when someone requested me as their trainer instead of one of my more athletic-looking peers.

What set me apart?

I cared.

Anyone can learn how to coach, but you can't teach giving a shit.

I never had to fake it as a trainer. I wanted more for my clients than they wanted for themselves, and it showed. It didn't matter if there was a snowstorm or I had to skip my own training—I was going to help each and every one of them. I still feel the same way today.

And my clients know I care about them. I like to joke that I care about them just a little more than they care about themselves. I've told them when they see only their set of footprints it's because I was carrying them. Maybe even more importantly, we have fun. I realized early on you can be the most amazing trainer in the world, but if your athletes are not enjoying themselves—laughing, high fiving, even hugging you—they won't come back.

Time and again, I would see other trainers' clients watching me with my client like sad puppies who hoped we would take them home. Other trainers were jealous. It was easier for them to blame me than figure out how they could improve. But I just went about my business, helping people get fitter and having fun in the process.

So, yeah, I'm not the most knowledgeable of trainers. If you're an athlete looking for the most comprehensive periodization program then I'm probably not your guy. But science is just one form of knowledge. I've learned a lot in my 25 years in the industry and I continue to learn more from not only empirical data, but from observing and listening to my athletes and clients. At the end of the day knowledge is useless if you don't know how to apply it, knowledge is potential power. The knowledge I have gained from taking the time to understand my clients' pain-points, their hopes and frustrations, has more than made-up for what I lack in exercise-science education.

Caring is how and why I emptied my bank account, and turned my last $500 into a successful affiliate that I later sold for $1 million and, more importantly, how I've managed to avoid having a "real" job my whole life. I'm not saying this to brag, but it's something I'm pretty damn proud of.

Let's be real: Whether you're a client, a trainer or a gym owner, people don't join a gym to get a sub-4 minute Fran or to deadlift 400 lbs. People want to be happy and healthy. They want to look better naked. More importantly, they often want to escape their troubles, whether it be a shitty job, screaming kids, or overbearing in-laws. All most people want is a one-hour reprieve, an outlet for their stress, that will extend their life and possibly get them abs - or maybe a muscle up - in the process.

As a rookie CrossFit-affiliate owner, this is what I failed to understand. I often focused on giving my members a second workout rather than being someone they could talk to. I made them do so many pull-ups that their hands ripped, rather than welcoming them into the community.

But I've learned. That's the purpose of this book: I want everyone to leave the gym thinking, "That workout was horrible. I can't wait to come back tomorrow!"

On these pages, I present lessons learned from owning three CrossFit affiliates, running CrossFit Games Regional competitions, judging CrossFit Games events and being part of CrossFit's Seminar Staff. Some of these lessons came quickly, others took years, and I'm still working on a handful. But each of them came from my unwavering desire to give people the best hour of their day.

*

When people ask me what it takes to run a successful affiliate, they want a simple answer. They're thinking of new programming or different class times or capping class sizes. Some of that would certainly help, but it wouldn't be enough. The lessons found in the following chapters are where the answers lie. They're up to you to implement. I encourage you to read one lesson per day—or maybe even per week—and think where, when and how you can put it to use at your affiliate, at home, at work, with your significant other and in everyday life.

These lessons not only helped me grow my affiliates but countless relationships. Most importantly, they helped me grow as a person.

Before you get started, here are two quick, tangible pieces of advice, if you're opening an affiliate or any small business:

1. Get a good accountant. When I first opened my gym, I knew nothing about business. I cheated and crammed my way through micro and macroeconomics. My "books" were a mess. And by "a mess," I mean I didn't track anything. I just bought stuff. It took me years to get my accounts in order for Uncle Sam. Had I not found a good accountant, I'd most likely be writing this book from the slammer.

2. Start small. You can always grow—be it space, schedule, equipment or staff. It's easy to add, hard to take

away. Start slowly and grow into it. You can get more equipment later, you can add another class to your schedule, you can develop the right coach. Running a new business is hard. Starting small will alleviate many of these stressors. You don't need to have everything on Day 1, and you don't need to appeal to everyone. It's OK to have a niche and it's OK to say "no." A quick way to end your small-business dreams is taking on too much and burning out.

Take those for what you will, but more importantly, know and follow your why. My why has always been about helping others, and that is what led me to writing this book.

Introduction

Before CrossFit

My fitness journey began on my first day of high school. Like any freshman, I was nervous heading into a new era of life. Three short years ago, I was the cool kid in elementary school. I had a girlfriend, was captain of my little league team and was always the first pick for sports in gym class. But by 7th grade, my life changed. I entered middle school, which comprised students from the six local elementary schools, and I was separated from my friends. I was placed in the smart-kid classes. It wasn't a bad thing. I just wasn't accustomed to hanging out with this crowd. I went from being lean and athletic to fat and nerdy.

My afternoons went from playing kickball and kill-the-carrier to working on math problems and playing video games. By the time I entered high-school, I was a full-blown chubby geek.

But that was about to end.

My high school was huge compared with my elementary and middle schools. I spent what seemed like hours walking around the hallways, trying to find my first class: Earth Science. I finally found the room after the bell rang.

"You're late," said the teacher, Mr. Ortega.

That rest of the hour seemed to go fine. But when the bell rang to end class, Mr. Ortega had his eyes on me.

"Ackerman, stay here for a minute."

"Great, I'm in trouble for being late to class," I thought. "My stepdad's going to punish me for this."

Instead, Mr. Ortega surprised me.

"I want you to join the wrestling team."

Unexpected.

I wasn't sure why he said this, but I was in. Looking back, it was a strange reaction. I didn't know much about wrestling. I had watched a few matches; a few of my buddies were on the team. Maybe even at 13, I knew something needed to change. All I thought about was girls; playing video games was not the best way to meet them.

I raced home and told my mom about my new athletic endeavor. I needed her to sign the permission slip. She was hesitant. She didn't want me to get hurt. I pleaded until she relented. Then she took me to the mall to buy my first pair of wrestling shoes.

Wrestling was a winter sport, so I had a few months to get back into shape. I talked with Mr. Ortega, who made it known why he wanted me to join the team. The lightest

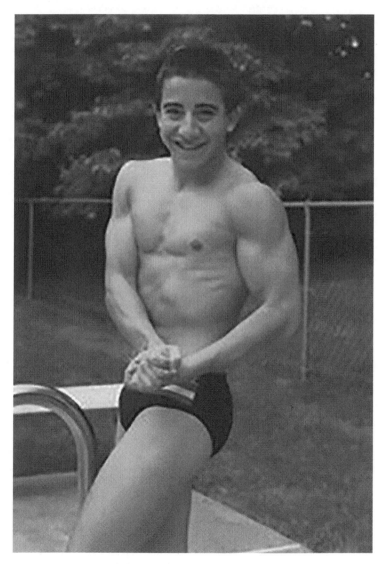

An overnight success 25 years in the making.

weight class at that time in New York was 91 lbs. For years, no one from my high school competed in that weight class. That meant every dual meet translated into a 6-point forfeit. Although I was only about 4-foot-10 at the time, I was nowhere near 91 lbs. I was closer to 120 lbs.

I had two months to lose 30 lbs. I had no idea how to do that. At that point in my life, my nutritional knowledge came from my divorced parents. My mom touted fat-free foods, while my dad vilified carbohydrates. I needed to know more. So, in those pre-internet days, I went to the library to search for books on weight loss and working out.

Armed with my new knowledge, a set of dumbbells and a rusty Schwinn stationary bike, I started my first training routine. I followed Arnold Schwarzenegger's "The New Encyclopedia of Modern Bodybuilding," as most teenage boys did back then. I did the best I could with my limited equipment. Most days I included hundreds of push-ups and sit-ups. My mom would yell from the kitchen, *"what's that noise"* as my body thumped against my bedroom floor rep after rep.

When November finally arrived, I showed up for my first practice unprepared. I had no idea the session would begin with a 3-mile warm-up run on the outdoor track. I had showed up in a T-shirt and shorts to run outside in winter in New York. To make matters worse, I finished the run last.

We returned to the wrestling room—also known as the school cafeteria—where the team gathered as Coach Ortega welcomed us to our first day. I looked around the room in awe. These were the superstars of the high school: Craig Glenn, the Salazzo twins, Mike Murphy. I couldn't believe I was hanging out with them. That fanboying was short lived after Coach Ortega blew the whistle and I spent the next three hours getting my ass kicked by those same kids.

While weightlifting had improved my physique, I was still the weakest person on the team and woefully unprepared for wrestling. This was my first lesson on functional fitness.

Each day after practice, the protocol was the same: roll up the mats, go to the locker room, step on the scale. Like everything in wrestling, there were standards:

1. Respect the scale.
2. Wipe off your feet.
3. Step on slowly.
4. Exhale your air.
5. Lean forward.

They were all tricks to get the scale to read a lighter weight.

I was the smallest and a lowly freshman, so I was the last one to step on the scale that first day.

"One hundred and ten pounds?" a shocked Coach Ortega said loudly and angrily.

The record skidded to a screeching halt as the entire team looked at me and laughed.

"I guess we still don't have a 91-pounder," Coach Ortega flatly said.

With my head down, I stepped off the scale, packed up my stuff and walked outside to wait for my mom to pick me up.

When she arrived, I got in the car and cried.

"I can't do this. Everyone is mean. And I'm 19 lbs. away from where I'm supposed to be."

My mom wasn't big on advice. But she was always supportive.

"You don't have to do this," she explained.

That's all I needed to hear. She was right: I didn't have to do this.

I slept like a baby that night. The next day, I would go to Earth Science class and tell Mr. Ortega I wasn't going to be part of the team.

When I woke up, I was nervous and stressed.

"Would he hate me? Yell at me? What would the team think of me?" I wondered.

As the first bell rang, I rehearsed in my head: "Mr. Ortega, wrestling just isn't for me. Thank you for the opportunity."

But that's not how it went. In fact, I didn't say anything. I went through the entire school day and showed up for Day 2 of wrestling practice.

It went on like this for weeks: I'd cry on the car ride home and commit to quitting, only to show up the next day and the one after that.

My mother was trying her best to be supportive, but her approach was to coddle me. Makes sense. As her only child, she just wanted me to be happy and feel safe. Little did she know she was influencing my mindset for my entire life. To this day, I don't thrive off of a you-can-do-it attitude. Sure, I'll take a high-five. I love the camaraderie of working out with others, but what really gets me amped is the notion that I'm not supposed to be able to do something. If others can't, I need to. My mom telling me it was OK to quit reinforced that it was not OK to quit.

Despite this newfound motivation, the scale still wasn't moving. I was even respecting it: wiping off my feet, stepping on slowly, exhaling my air and leaning forward.

But each time, Coach Ortega would set the scale at 91 lbs. only to watch it forcefully tip to the left until he slid the indicator one pound at a time to 110 lbs.

By now it was early December. Our first match of the year was quickly approaching. I had been doing well at practice, working on my shooting and half nelsons, and gaining confidence. But I knew it didn't matter. I wouldn't wrestle. The team included a bunch of studs at the 105-lbs. and 112-lbs. weight classes. Even at my current weight, I wasn't good enough.

That's when it finally happened.

Practice ended. Per usual, I stepped on the scale. Once again, Coach Ortega set it at 91 lbs. The scale tipped again. But as he slid the indicator higher, it stopped at 100 lbs. I had lost 10 lbs.!

Coach Ortega looked at me stoically.

"Maybe you can make 91 pounds."

I looked over at Pete. Pete was a savage. He and his twin brother, Jason, were beasts. They wrestled at 98 and 119 lbs., respectively. Pete smirked at Coach Ortega's remark. Pete was my practice buddy along with the 105-lbs. Luke, Coach Ortega's son. Those two were relentless. They kicked my ass every day. I knew I didn't stand a chance against Pete. My goal remained the 91-lbs. weight class.

With one week before that first match, the scale kept showing weight loss. I was closing in on that elusive 91 lbs. But the night before the first match, I weighed 93 lbs.

"It's over," I thought. "I failed."

Coach Ortega had other plans.

"Go home. Don't eat, don't drink, and tomorrow you will make weight."

"Was he serious?" I wondered. "No food or even water?"

I agreed to Coach Ortega's plan, but I couldn't tell my mom. She'd lose her mind. A Jewish mother allowing her son to go hungry? Sacrilegious! When I got home, I told my mom I'd eat dinner in my room and quickly fed the meatloaf to the dog.

Looking back, a 12-hour fast isn't a big deal. I've done several three and seven-day fasts since then. But at the time, that was like telling me I'd never eat again. I don't know how I did it or even why, but I made it through the night without sneaking downstairs for a snack. The next day, I got ready for school, went to the locker room to weigh in for the meet.

Like usual, Coach Ortega set the scale at 91 lbs. I stepped on. This time, it didn't tip.

I had done it. I had made weight! I was officially a member of the varsity wrestling team.

After I stepped off the scale, I sat down next to my locker and ate the peanut-butter-and-banana sandwich my mom had made me for breakfast. Coach Ortega took a seat next to me.

"Nice job," he said.

I was hooked.

Later that afternoon—after getting pinned in 19 seconds—I learned that making weight was only half the battle. I still needed to learn how to wrestle. While I'd love to tell you I quickly learned how to shoot the baddest double leg on the planet and went on to win the state tournament, that's not how things went. I proceeded to lose every match for the next three months. I found myself on my back, looking up at the lights three times a week in front of my team, my peers and the fans who had come to watch. By now, making weight was easier. I was walking around at 91 lbs. and didn't have to go without eating anymore. But the stress was wearing on me. I'd have nightmares about meets. I'd think about them all day until the referee blew the whistle to start the match and blew it again to signify I had, once again, been pinned.

This went on the entire season until our final match of the season.

My record was 0-17. I had been pinned in 15 of those losses and was only able to endure the entire 6 minutes twice. Needless to say, I was happy the season was ending. I had survived. I was ready to accept this last pin and retire from wrestling. As I was about to step on the mat for the last time, Coach Ortega pulled me aside.

"Do your best," he said.

At hearing those simple words, I felt relaxed. I realized I had been so stressed with making weight and trying to be on the team that I wasn't being the best me.

I ran onto the mat, stepped on the line, shook my opponent's hand and shot in for a double leg the instant the whistle blew. I took him down, put on a half nelson, rolled him to his back and pinned him. In 12 seconds—a record that still stands as the fastest pin at my high school.

I jumped up, fists held high as if I had just won an Olympic gold medal. My teammates gathered around me and celebrated. It was the first match of the meet, so the celebration was short lived. But I sat on the bench feeling elated while everyone else competed.

What's most significant about my first wrestling season wasn't that I made the varsity team or that I was hanging out with the cool kids or even that I won that one match. It was that at 13, I was able to change my mindset and overcome obstacles.

After that final match, practice went on for my teammates who continued to sectional and state tournaments. I showed up for practice to help out and be a good drilling partner. I was the only freshman still going to practice with the varsity team. It was after one of those practices that I headed to the locker room to find my teammates waiting for me. They gathered around me and started clapping.

"Ackerman, we tried to get you to quit from Day 1," Pete said. "But you kept showing up. We're not sure why. You kept getting your ass kicked, but you made it."

He shook my hand and presented me with my varsity letter.

That moment is etched in my memory as a reminder that no matter what is coming at me, I can persevere.

As an adult I frequently call on that period of my life as a motivational reminder. If I can demonstrate that level of grit as a nerdy high-schooler, then what's stopping me now!? It usually does the trick in getting me fired up and helps me overcome whatever obstacle is in the way.

By the time my sophomore wrestling season ended, I had earned more of my teammates' respect as a solid competitor and finished with All Section honors. The summer practices and the weight training had paid off.

As my high-school years went on, I continued to develop, progressing from someone ready to quit on Day 1 to a well-respected—and even feared—wrestler in our area. I stayed at that 91-lbs. weight class through my junior year, which meant lots of hungry nights but I continued to tirelessly train.

After my junior year, I was one match away from winning the Sectional tournament when I realized I just couldn't keep up with the weight cutting. I was 17 years old and still withering my body down to double digits. Three years of such extreme measures had taken its toll on me. After that season ended, I talked to my coach and we agreed I needed to move up to the 105-lb. weight class.

The first day after my junior-year season, I hit the weights hard at Club Fit. That spring, I put on over 25 lbs. of muscle. I spent hours training every day. I'd train, go home, eat and go back to train more.

I spent so much time there, I became close with Mike, one of the trainers. At the time, I considered 28-year-old Mike omniscient. He was at the gym 24/7 either working out or training clients. Mike grew to like me and in no time, I was training with him.

The first time I trained with him involved back squats, hack squats, leg extensions, leg press and what seemed like thousands of calf raises. I had trouble keeping up, but tried to put on a brave face so Mike wouldn't see how much I was suffering.

The next morning, I could barely get myself out of bed, much less to the toilet. The soreness was agonizing. Sitting was brutal. Yet, I loved it. That feeling of being sore is still something I love. From that first day of wrestling practice to my first real training session, I loved the feeling of getting the most out of my body, knowing I made it stronger.

Then I found out about delayed onset muscle soreness (DOMS), when you're more sore the second and third day after training than the first. Long story short: It took me more than a week to recover from that leg day. When Mike asked me to join again, you know I was ready!

This was my mentality at the gym: You were there to give it 110 percent.

By my senior year, I wasn't only training regularly, I was interning at the gym through my high school's program that allowed 10 of us to leave early for real-world experience. The other nine kids shadowed doctors, lawyers and veterinarians. I was at the gym.

Training others was becoming my passion. I wanted to learn everything I could about working out.

Before long, Joe, the gym manager, let me lead intro sessions and train clients.

That semester was amazing. I was in school for second and third periods, then I spent the rest of my day at the gym learning, training and coaching. I was preparing for the rest of my life, though I didn't realize it at the time.

High-School graduation came and I went off to college. After my freshman year at the University of Albany, SUNY, I headed back home for summer. I was itching to get back to training at Club Fit. With a personal-trainer certification under my belt, the gym offered me my first real position as a personal trainer.

Once my senior year rolled around, I lived off campus and expanded my experience with jobs at just about every gym in town. The highlight was becoming a personal trainer at Gold's Gym, where I worked my way up to manager within a year. As my friends were sending out résumés and getting their internships ready for the next chapter of their lives, I was still doing bicep curls and growing my list of clients.

When I graduated in 2000, I didn't know much except that I didn't want a "real job." My friends all had those: real-estate agents, doctors, attorneys, financial investors. I was still teaching spin and yoga at the local YMCA. I was basically a glorified aerobics instructor with pay so meager I had to move to the worst part of downtown Albany, New York.

So, there I was, living in the ghetto as a college graduate. My friends were moving to New York City, Long Island and Westchester for jobs earning six figures and I was living next door to the "smelly deli" and surviving on ramen.

But the flexible schedule was great. I was exercising every day, and wearing a tank top and shorts to work. Who cares if I was driving a 20-year-old car and a fancy date night consisted of taking my girlfriend out to Subway? We were eating fresh, and I was doing what I loved: helping people.

I loved the feeling of inspiring someone to be better. That's more than my friends could say, as they were constantly complaining about their bosses, the workload, and, of course, the stock market. Still, it was difficult to ignore my $8-an-hour pay coupled with working 12-hour days. I could barely pay my rent. My then-girlfriend wasn't amused. Her friends were talking about new, hip restaurants and weekend getaways, but all she ever heard was, "Six-inch or footlong?"

I was more educated than the people running the gym but earning less. Still, it was my passion. From the moment I walked into a gym as a high-school freshman, I had found my calling. I loved the training, the smell of the gym and that feeling of pushing my body past its boundaries. It was me.

When my girlfriend gave me an ultimatum—get a real job or go get a new girlfriend—I called up my best lifting partner and asked if he wanted to squat. As much as I was frustrated, tired and broke, I just couldn't bring myself to get a "real job." I looked at ads, even went on a few interviews. I couldn't pull the trigger.

But just like in any good movie, I had my protagonist's moment.

As usual, my alarm clock went off at 4 a.m. Monday. I set it for that time so I could make it to the gym by 5 a.m. I either had spin class, boot camp or a client to train. My days were long, typically starting at 5 a.m. and ending around 9 p.m.

I loved teaching spin. But my fellow aerobics instructors didn't like me. I was a young male who was stirring trouble with my rock music to the merriment of those on the waiting list to get into my class.

On this particular day, I dragged my ass out of bed, downed an energy drink, grabbed my gym bag and headed to the door. I was excited about the new playlist I had made. I knew my 5 a.m. Monday class was going to be jam packed and high energy.

16

I opened my front door. As I made my way to my car, I saw the silhouette of someone sitting in my front seat. It was early and my brain was foggy. It took me a minute to understand what I was seeing: Yes, someone had broken into my car. The perpetrator and I made eye contact. I discerned his "oh shit" facial expression as if to say, "What kind of lunatic is up at this hour?"

I turned around, went back inside my apartment and called the police. The police arrived within minutes, but it was too late. My stereo was gone, and I was left with a busted car window.

I made it to class on time, driving in the dead of winter with no passenger window, and still had a blast teaching thanks to my amazing new playlist and awesome clients. But something had to give.

I was content, I had a girlfriend, my own place, and a job I loved. But I was not challenging myself. I lived in the worst part of town, earned next to nothing and had very little prospect of career advancement. Where was I going? I had no idea.

So, I went back to school to pursue my master's degree in psychology. Fitness, I figured, wouldn't cut it for the rest of my life.

The decision to go back to school led me to make other changes, including increasing my personal-training rates, asking for raises at all of my globo-gym jobs, and being smarter and selective about which shifts I accepted.

Slowly, my mindset about work changed, as did my bank account. Within a year, I was able to move out of that ghetto apartment and buy my first house. The decision to make a change significantly impacted the direction of my life.

Turns out the guy stealing my stereo was a huge motivator for me. I'm not sure I'd be where I am today without him. Thank you, and I hope you enjoy that stereo as much as I did.

*

I first heard about CrossFit in 2006 from my buddy Chad at Brazilian Jiu Jitsu. He showed me the latest issue of Muscle & Fitness magazine with MMA champion Chuck Liddell doing this new exercise routine called CrossFit. I immediately went home and jumped on the internet to learn more.

There wasn't much: just a bare-bones website, CrossFit. com, with a brutal workout of the day (WOD) posted. There was a language and culture to this site unlike any I'd seen. People commented on every workout and shared their experiences of suffering. I had no idea where to begin. So, I decided there was no time like the present. I'd just follow the daily WOD.

That next day, Sunday, I began implementing CrossFit into my workout routine. This particular WOD offered a choice between two named workouts: Cindy or Mary. The latter included handstand push-ups and pistols—neither of which I could do, so I chose Cindy. It called for as many rounds as possible in 20 minutes of 5 pull-ups, 10 push-ups and 15 air squats.

Less than 8 minutes into Cindy, I found myself gasping for air. I had gone from doing 5 pull-ups unbroken to one at a time and was failing push-ups. People at Gold's Gym were looking at me like I was a lunatic. And I had to fend off bodybuilders from the cable-crossover machine I was using for its pull-up bar.

This workout humbled me. It reminded me of my first day of wrestling practice. I went home that day to do more research on CrossFit. I learned about scaling, kipping pull-ups and midline stabilization. When I wasn't

Marvin Maldonado, Renzo Gracie, Jason Ackerman.

training CrossFit, I was learning everything I could about it. I became a vocal part of the forum and even a moderator, communicating with CrossFit Founder Greg Glassman, Lynne Pitts, Josh Murphy and a few other OGs.

I followed CrossFit.com for the next month, hitting every workout posted. I had to scale many movements because I couldn't do them or didn't have the proper equipment: towel pull-ups for rope climbs, sumo deadlift high-pulls for rowing.

The Court Club, home to many of my first CrossFit workouts.

The first time I saw the workout Isabel posted, the instructions read:

"For time:

Snatch 135 pounds, 30 reps

Use 95 pounds, 65 pounds or broomstick as needed."

I laughed.

"Who can't move 135 pounds?" I wondered.

Turns out I couldn't. I quickly learned to leave my ego at the door.

When I did a workout such as Fight Gone Bad, I would run all over the gym using equipment.

People started asking questions:

"What are you doing?"

"Are you going to hurt yourself?"

"Aren't those cheating pull-ups?"

"Can I do it?"

CrossFit entered my life at the perfect time—like a neon sign from up above with bells, whistles and singing angels. At that time, I was ready to leave the fitness world. I couldn't keep scraping by, unsure if I'd be able to pay my next utility bill. By this time, I had a master's in psychology and was going to get a "real job", like school psychologist or guidance counselor—something that included normal hours, a regular paycheck and maybe even some benefits.

That's why CrossFit saved me. It stopped me from joining the traditional working world and kept me doing what I loved: helping people. From that first workout, I knew I had stumbled on something special and that it had the power to change my life.

So, I took the $500 I'd saved over seven years—and a credit card with a $2,000 limit—took my CrossFit Level 1 Certificate Course and then opened Albany CrossFit in 2007.

I was now a business owner. I was proud of myself. I was doing something. I was no longer relying on other people. I was responsible for myself. If I made money or didn't, it was going to be because of me. It was exhilarating—like an injection of B12 straight to my heart. I was reborn.

As the days, weeks and months passed, I realized I was not merely a business owner but an influencer. I knew I was helping people when I was doing one-on-one training. But I viewed it superficially: They look better, so they are happier. I soon learned CrossFit wasn't just a workout, it was a way of life. These clients were becoming friends with one another, exchanging numbers, having get-togethers and slowly becoming a family. I was creating a community.

CrossFit opened my eyes to my true passion: Helping others be the best version of themselves. That is my "why." Slowly but surely, those same middle-aged women that I could barely get to do a set of leg extensions were getting fit. They were deadlifting, snatching, and squatting. Imagine my surprise and pride as I watched them achieve their first pull-up. It was so much more than I ever dreamed they could do. The change was no longer superficial. They exuded confidence. It was then that I began to realize it was just as important for me to help them understand their "why" as it was for me to understand mine.

*

Having a strong "why" and letting it guide me is what has kept me doing what I love my entire life. It's what kept me battling through the tough times, overcoming obstacle after obstacle, and ultimately led me to my success. When times were tough, when challenging decisions had to be made, it was easy, because it always came down to my values: health, happiness, passion and helping others.

Years later, after selling my affiliates, my "why" continues to be my compass. While many aspects of my life have changed, my desire to help others has not. It's the reason I continue to travel every weekend to teach CrossFit Inc. seminars, hop on a phone call whenever a client needs to talk or respond to emails from affiliate owners seeking to improve their business.

For me, it was always about helping others. It's what stopped me from quitting my job at the gym whenever my parents badgered me or my girlfriend complained about our crappy apartment.

Our "why" guides us. It keeps us headed in the right direction. If you don't know yours or, worse yet, you don't live by yours, you won't be successful. Sure, you might have a great job, or all the money you need, but if your life is not aligned with your "why," you won't be happy.

Do you know your significant other's "why," your family's, your friends', your coaching staff's? Do you know what drives them? Ever get into a heated argument to realize neither of you is bending on your beliefs—clearly because you were being driven by your "why?"

One of my favorite activities has grown to be sitting down with anyone and understanding their core values and their "why." As I started doing that with my loved ones, coaches and even strangers, it allowed me to be a better friend, partner, business owner, leader and human being.

I remember sitting down with Dean, one of my coaches, about his absence on Sundays at the gym. We had a lot of weekend activities at Albany CrossFit; it was the best time to build our community as athletes from various classes came together. But it seemed like no matter how much I asked Dean to be there, he wasn't. We were both frustrated with one another, and it was showing in his coaching and in my leadership.

When yet another Sunday event came and went without Dean, I was furious. As I often did at the time, I pulled out my phone and shot him a nasty text that we needed to chat right away about this. The next day, we sat down.

24

I truly liked Dean; we often had deep conversations. This meeting started off that way. We started talking about religion—nothing too deep; just our backgrounds and current practices. I knew Dean was religious—whatever that meant—but it wasn't until this chat that I understood just how important his faith was to him and his wife. He had coached for me for almost a year, and I had no idea. I learned that Sundays were a day he spent in church with family. It was a lightbulb moment for me. Now I understood why he was never around on Sundays. We both left that meeting feeling better about the situation.

Celebrating at Dean and Savanah's wedding.

Dean later opened his own affiliate to tremendous success but eventually sold it. When I asked him about it, his "why" came shining through.

"I was here one day from 5 a.m. to 10 p.m., and I looked over at the couch and envisioned my daughter asleep on it, and I thought to myself, I don't want that for her," Dean told me. "I want her at home with me there to do homework and to tuck her in at night."

This was a man who stuck to his "why." Faith and family were his guiding tenets, so much so that he sold a successful business because it didn't align with his values.

Do you have a "why?" A burning desire inside of you? A guiding truth that leads you through obstacles and barriers so you know you're making the right decision?

Define your "why"—find it and live by it. It represents the knowledge, understanding and power that comes with realizing you're in control. You are in charge of you.

Before I found CrossFit, I was being influenced by everyone around me. No one—not one person—encouraged me to stay in the world of fitness. But I did anyway. Don't listen to anyone else. Listen to yourself and what you know to be true. Trust your gut. Follow your "why."

*

Without further ado, here are 30 lessons I've learned over the years. Some of these lessons came quickly, others took years, and I am grateful for each one. I hope my mistakes can help you lead a better life and help you provide for others the best hour of their day.

Lesson 1

Go All In

*"If you do what you've always done, you'll
get what you've always gotten."*
—JESSIE POTTER

With Coach Glassman.

CrossFit comes into my life and right away it's a game-changer. I loved the workouts, and I loved the idea of starting my own gym. Since my first day at Club Fit, my goal was to open a gym. I even started a notebook detailing what it would look like, what machines I would buy, where the pool would be. Hey, if you're going to dream, dream big.

As I got older, I knew this dream would cost far more money than I had. But CrossFit was different—I could afford this. There were no machines or pools or saunas at a CrossFit affiliate. It was unlike any gym I had seen. I didn't quite have enough money, but I was able to open one credit card that would help me afford it. While I was in love with this idea and knew I needed a change, it still took me nearly a year to pull the trigger and open my first business. I waffled. I made pros-and-cons lists and spreadsheets, I talked with every business owner I encountered, and I spent endless hours debating whether I could—or should—do this.

As I was talking with my aunt, a successful businesswoman, she told me CrossFit espoused a bad business model.

"You can't open a gym and actually want people to show up," she explained. "You need to charge less and hope they don't come in."

Little did she know this was the standard gym model.

I was confused, anxious and nervous. I was also broke. But I had no other path in sight.

Do you ever find yourself stalling to make a decision?

Perhaps it involves ending a relationship, creating a new habit or starting a new exercise routine.

I was the worst with decisions—from opening this business to what toaster to buy. I would spend hours and days researching a choice only to realize I was never truly satisfied. Nowadays, I have learned to pick one and move on. Like getting in a pool, I have found it's better to jump in than inch in one toe at a time. Cannonball!

I found my point of no return when I emailed Nicole Carroll, who today helps lead CrossFit Inc.'s Training Department. Nicole was in nearly every video CrossFit.com published and seemed to oversee all of the affiliates, at the time. Just drafting an email to her sent panic through my body; getting a quick response made me feel special—like hearing back from a celebrity.

At the time, there was a single CrossFit Level 1 Certificate Course each weekend—if that—and most of the courses had been sold out for weeks. Nicole said if I committed today, she could squeeze me in to the L1 in Toronto, Canada. I used my credit card to immediately pay for the $1,000 course. I would also need to charge the gas for the 16-hour round-trip drive to Toronto, the three nights in a hotel room and my affiliate fee. Luckily for me, the affiliate fee was only $500 at the time. Today, it's upward of $3,000.

Group photo from my L1 in Toronto, Canada.

At that point, I started picking out equipment, investigating places to lease, and I started training more people to save money for my next venture.

In cognitive psychology, there is the concept of loss aversion: the tendency to prefer avoiding losses rather than equivalent gains. For example, would you rather not lose $20 than find $20? We see this all the time when it comes to money. We view money loss twice as powerfully, psychologically, than equal financial gain.

This is to say that once I put in that $1,000, I was going to do anything not to lose it. Even if that meant borrowing $500 from my girlfriend who had a good job and made more than double what I did. In the years we dated I never asked her for money; I would have been embarrassed. Now I felt differently. I needed to do this. I borrowed the money.

Making an investment is often times the best way to hit your goal. But it doesn't have to cost $1,000 and require you to borrow money from your significant other. It can be a barter, a time investment or even an agreement you make with someone to hold each other accountable.

You have to put yourself in a position where there is no turning back if you truly want to accomplish great things. The truth is, had I not charged that $1,000 and driven 16 hours over the border, chances are I'd still be a personal trainer and group-aerobics instructor. I'd be the old, disgruntled globo-gym trainer wearing Zubaz pants, a tank top and a fanny pack, gripping to my youth while chasing after young aerobics instructors. I'd be living alone on Ramen and protein shakes. It would be sad.

Don't get me wrong: I was scared. I didn't know how I'd get members or if I'd ever pay myself. I should have paid closer attention in microeconomics class. One thing I did know: This was happening. I was in the deep end. It was sink or swim.

That approach turned out to be a notable lesson in my life and a tactic I continue to use.

Whether the investment causes me to step up, many times it's simply the act of making the investment. A recent example: I had decided to get my own business coach. The one I chose cost $10,000. Crazy talk. Once again, faced with such a big financial implication, I found myself waffling. Should I or shouldn't I? Can I afford him? Was it worth it?

The goal of hiring a business coach was to better myself and improve how I run my businesses. Truth is, it wasn't the financial investment that mattered but the fact that he was in my life to help me grow, therefore I would. When I hired him, it changed what I did every morning because I wanted to be that person he was coaching me to be. It changed multiple aspects of my behavior, including how I interacted with people, what time I went to bed and what time I woke up. Without the financial implication, I wouldn't be working half as hard.

We all know those members with whom you're a bit too generous. Maybe you give them a free month because they couldn't afford their membership. Then, they don't show up. That's because they're no longer invested. It's easier for members who aren't paying to put in less effort. It's why I always charge everyone—it's not for me, it's for them. Plus, nothing makes me madder than being generous with a member only to see them posting pictures of sushi dinners and expensive glasses of wine on social media.

So, an investment isn't defined by spending every last dollar you have—like I did—but by forcing yourself to act.

Be it small or large, financial or emotional, an investment forces you to have skin in the game to help you take yourself to your goal.

That weekend of my CrossFit L1 seminar changed my life. I was already in love with CrossFit, but meeting some of my CrossFit heroes was surreal. These were true-life web-lebrities—before Instagram existed. These were people I had watched do the same workouts as me but way better.

They were all there: Nicole Carroll, Annie Sakamoto and Eva Twardokens.

Then-Seminar Staff member Jon Gilson talked to me about equipment purchases: "Thirty-fives are dumb. Your

Albany CrossFit early 2008.

35

money is better spent on buying more 25s and 10s, as most Rx workouts require those."

Pat Sherwood helped me with my muscle-up, watching as I kipped myself over the rings so that the sunglasses holding back my hair flipped forward and landed perfectly in place.

"Look at the cool guy hitting muscle-ups."

And Dave Castro taught the GHD lecture. Before he was "The Dave Castro," he was just another badass L1 instructor.

My personal favorite was Nicole yelling at me during Tabata squats: "Come on, Jason. You can do more."

We worked out and worked out some more. I PRd my Fran time and made friends for life. All because I invested.

Funny story: This was my first time doing CrossFit with others, and I thought I was good. We were each given a judge for the workout. I looked at mine and proudly stated, "I'm probably going to finish in under 8 minutes." I thought I was a big deal. I was neck and neck with someone right in front of me, who suddenly stopped.

"This guy quit the workout, really?" I thought.

Turned out he was a round ahead of me and finished minutes before I did. That's when I learned an 8-minute Fran wasn't so impressive.

If you own an affiliate, chances are you've had an all-in moment. Or maybe it's why you started CrossFit. Something made you act.

If you're thinking about opening a box or making a big change in your life, what can you do right now to help yourself act? To make that investment?

As the L1 seminar was ending, Coach Greg Glassman was shaking everyone's hands and hugging participants. I walked up to him and asked, "What should I do to run a successful affiliate?"

I saw the sincerity in his eyes as he looked at me and offered one word: "Care."

I was all in.

Lesson 2

We Fail at the Margins of Our Experiences

"If you ever travel back in time, don't step on anything because even the tiniest change can alter the future in ways you can't imagine."
—Grandpa Simpson

My mentor Sasa once asked me, "What would you prefer: comfort or discomfort?"

It wasn't a trick question, and the answer is obvious. As human beings, we seek comfort. Given the option between the bed and the floor, or eating and going hungry, most of us would choose the bed and eating.

But Sasa wasn't done. He paused and re-phrased the question: "Would you rather comfort or growth?"

With the Mirkovic family, Sasa, Kosta, Stella, Oscar, and Laura.

Now I had to think.

Of course, I still wanted comfort. But I only get one life. I wanted to grow and evolve, so I answered "growth."

Yes, I still wanted a bed, and I still wanted to eat. But, at other times, I needed to seek out growth rather than just doing what made me comfortable.

That being said, you need to stay safe. Imagine yourself looking out over the edge of the Grand Canyon. As you get closer to the edge, your heart rate increases just a bit and, if you get too close, it jumps rapidly. It's your body's way of saying, "Hey, dummy, you could fall off and die." That's not what I'm talking about here. Get yourself away from the edge; don't be an idiot.

What I *am* referencing are those times in life when you can stay put and do what you've always done, or challenge yourself and maybe, just maybe, come out better on the other side.

- Your job is comfortable, but you want to open a box?
- You want to participate in a competition, but it's scary?
- You want to ask out your crush, but you fear rejection?
- You want to wake up early, but you hit the snooze button?

These are small examples of when we should leave our comfort zones.

There is a saying about the magic in life happens outside your comfort zone. How many memorable moment can you think of that happened on your couch, other than making out with your highschool sweetheart? Think about how many amazing experiences you have had simply because you chose to get uncomfortable. Usually it's accompanied by nerves, butterflies, a lump in your throat. Afterwards, though, it's exhilarating. You feel amazing. It is truly what life is all about.

In late 2006, when I was about ready to quit the fitness industry and get a "real job," I found CrossFit. At first, it was just a new, more fun way of training. And then I started implementing it with my clients. But it wasn't until I was on a long bike ride with my friend Susie that I realized it could actually become a career. Susie was a client of mine and loved my spin classes. She was a regular and eventually got so involved in spin that she started biking outdoors. She went on some epic trips across the United States, through Canada and even toured France—all because she decided to take up spinning.

While out biking on our standard loop around Vorheesville and Guilderland, there was always this one harrowing climb. It was just over 3 miles and boasted an incline that made you question gravity. It took nearly 30 minutes of grinding to make it to the top. But when you did, the view was stunning. We had made it to the top, as we had dozens of times before, and Susie said, "You need to do something with yourself. You are too good to be wasting your time teaching spin and aerobics and training people like me one on one." Her words hit me hard. Stung, actually.

"Who is she to tell me what I should or shouldn't be doing," I thought.

But knowing Susie, I knew she said them with the best of intentions.

At the time, I had no way of knowing her words would change my life.

She was right. Susie had always been a straight-shooter with me. Whether it was women I was dating, pushing harder on the bike or my career path, I could always count on her to challenge me, physically and emotionally. We all need a Susie in our lives.

Her words were all I could think about for the rest of the ride. How could I find a place to rent? How could I afford to pay for my CrossFit L1 seminar? How would I get more clients? All fair questions, and all reasons I knew I had to open my own gym.

I had three choices: train people at globo gyms, get out of the fitness industry or do this new and exciting thing called CrossFit. I chose CrossFit, even though it scared the shit out of me.

The rest, as they say, is history.

As I mentioned earlier, I emptied my bank account and opened Albany CrossFit. What I didn't mention is where I opened.

At that time, I was training a who's who of the area. During a training session with one of my clients who was a successful real-estate agent, I asked him to help me find a location. I described my requirements: an open-floor space, high ceilings for wall-ball shots and rope climbs, and plumbing for a shower. Barry took a moment to think and then said, "no." I was a bit mad. This was his job, after all.

"Go ask the owner of this building if you can rent one of the racquetball courts here," Barry replied.

Mind. Blown.

Back then, I was doing most of my training in an outdated facility called The Court Club. Built in 1978, the gym sported shag carpet and lime-green tiles, and had all the naked old men you would care to see. At one point, it must have been the hippest place in town—outfitted with a bar and restaurant, and 18 racquetball, handball, and squash courts. What Barry and I both knew is all of those sports were dying. Most of the time, those courts would idly sit in the dark. Barry was certain the owner, Shye, would allow me to rent one.

I approached Shye about this idea and, as was his style, he took a few days to think it over. He eventually agreed to let me rent a court for $800 per month. We shook hands and that was it—no written agreements or lawyers. I was officially opening my first gym.

What's funny is that as I stepped out of my comfort zone and into the world of business ownership, it wasn't just my bank account that changed. I slowly grew as a person, too. Without having done this, I wouldn't have met the people I have known, become a better coach, become a boss or even met my wife. And it was all from that chat with Susie at the top of Thatcher Park.

Life isn't always comfortable. But if you continue to rise, to meet new challenges headlong, to face your weaknesses and to step outside your comfort zone, you will become the best version of yourself.

(Clockwise from top) Group picture from one of the first workouts at Albany CrossFit; my early days of coaching, please excuse the cargo pants; one of my long-time clients Dona; Susie hitting her first CrossFit workout.

Lesson 3

Life is a Series of Dips

"The things you think about determine the quality of your mind. Your soul takes on the color of your thoughts."
—Marcus Aurelius

What they don't tell you about opening your first business is your friends will eventually leave you.

I had a hard time drawing the line between friends and clients. It's something I still struggle with. As Steve Carrell's "The Office" character Michael Scott said, "Why don't I tell you what my greatest weaknesses are? I work too hard, I care too much, and sometimes I can be too invested in my job."

I would estimate that in my time as an affiliate owner, I gave out over five years worth of free memberships, and I wouldn't change that. Just maybe who I gave them to.

The beauty of CrossFit gyms is they're part of an affiliate system, not a franchise. As such, there are a lot of gray areas. Sometimes your clients and coaching staff can see this as opportunities. Who can fault them? They see your wonderful life and want the same. They do "member math:" There are 100 members, everyone is paying $200 a month; therefore, Jason is making $20,000 a month. In all seriousness, coaching for a living is awesome. You're doing something you love—changing people's lives—in shorts and a T-shirt. Of course they want in on the action. Who can blame them?

One of my first members at Albany CrossFit was Jess. She was a friend. We had gone on a date or two in the past and really bonded over the TV show "Lost." We had weekly screening parties that only got bigger once the affiliate was up and running.

Jess came in on the second Monday the box was open to do the Filthy 50 workout at the encouragement of my longtime one-on-one client, John. He was obsessed with CrossFit and wouldn't shut up about it.

Earlier that day, Dave, a 65-year-old attorney with two children in their late 30s and two others in diapers, also did his first WOD. Needless to say, he was a young and vibrant 65, so I treated him as such. Minutes after he finished, he passed out on the gym floor. Not like, "I'm tired and going to lie down." He fainted. I had taken enough CPR classes to know I needed to call 911. As paramedics were loading him onto the ambulance for precautionary measures, Dave looked at me, smiled and said, "Sign me up."

Like Dave, Jess gave it her all. She was an avid runner and looked great in those early minutes, crushing the box jumps, jumping pull-ups and walking lunges. But as the workout stretched past the 20-minute mark, Jess turned pale. Her eyes rolled back in her head, and down she went.

"Two for two," I thought.

Since she was in her early 20s, I wasn't quite as concerned as I had been with Dave. Jess woke up a few seconds later and we gave her some sugar water—aka Gatorade—and she quickly got over her embarrassment.

People either love CrossFit immediately or never come back.

Jess did not let that experience keep her from coming back. She showed up the next day. Later, she ended up becoming the first Albany CrossFit member of the month.

Together, Jess and John were a dream team. Before long, we had all four of Jess's sisters, her mom, aunt and most of the downtown-Troy 30-somethings coming to the box. Business was booming. This was my first sign I was onto something big. Up until that point, Albany CrossFit members were longtime clients and friends. Now I was attracting people I hadn't previously met. They would call or stop in and ask, "Is this that crazy workout where people pass out?"

Jess was totally invested. Within a few months she got her L1 certificate and started coaching part-time. The first time I went away on a vacation, Jess covered my classes. She also organized the first party at the box. At one point, she was even programming workouts. And that was all before she even got her first pull-up.

Funny sidebar: We had this other member, Ben. Crude as fuck and unapologetic about it. Ben was a retired Marine. His language was rough, his demeanor was tough and he was covered in tribal tattoos. He was a good guy—the kind you want on your side. A bunch of us went out to a hibachi dinner. Jess and Ben were both there. When the night was over, Jess told me how much she disliked Ben's vulgar humor. Long story short: They were engaged within a year. I was given the honor of being the best man at their wedding.

Here's where this story goes awry. Box owners, you'll understand.

Jess was my best member and a great friend, so it came as a complete shock to me about a year later when she sat me down and told me she wanted to open her own box.

I was enraged.

"How could she? What does she know? That backstabber!" I thought.

With Katie Lasky at Jess and Ben's wedding.

It was the first box to open from under my umbrella—now there have been over 50—and I didn't know how to handle it. To say I handled it poorly is an understatement.

I fired Jess.

Right there on the spot. No questions asked, no talking about it.

"You're fired."

I told her she couldn't work out there anymore. I immediately took her pictures off our website. I told the other coaches there was to be no contact with her.

I was outraged. I thought of everything that was going to go wrong now. I was only concerned with how many of our members we would lose because of Jess. I was not the least bit grateful or appreciative of what she'd done for the community. To this day, I am embarrassed by my actions.

There are more than 1 billion people on this planet and over 200,000 where we lived. We were not competing over

With my first four female coaches and Coach Glassman, from left to right, Viv, Joy, Jess, and Niki.

50

the 200 that already did CrossFit. Our job was—and is—to educate the masses on the importance of activity. There is plenty to go around.

These days, as I travel and meet box owners and coach them, I remind them that a true sign of how well they are doing is how many boxes opened from within them. How many people can say you've shown them that they can open their own business? That they can take control of their destiny?

Remember, introspection begets wisdom. How you react will dictate your happiness.

It took a long time for Jess's and my relationship to recover. I had gone from being the best man at her wedding to an enemy.

Nearly two years later at a local competition, our paths crossed again. We smiled, hugged and apologized to each other for how we had handled the situation and for allowing it to interfere with our friendship. I'm glad to say we remain friends to this day and opening her affiliate was not only able to change her life but help thousands of others who weren't already exposed to CrossFit. Most of her sisters also became coaches, and she and Ben have two wonderful children.

Great job, Jess. I'm proud of you.

Lesson 4

The Rule is
The Rule

"Don't expect to be motivated every day to get out there and make things happen. You won't be. Don't count on motivation. Count on discipline."
— JOCKO WILLINK

Owning your own business is amazing.

You don't have a true boss, you can set your own schedule, the pay doesn't have a ceiling, and you get to make the rules.

Owning your own business also is challenging.

You don't have a true boss, you can set your own schedule, the pay doesn't have a ceiling, and you get to make the rules.

The reason I love owning my own businesses is the freedom. But how I defined freedom in 2007 is far different than I do now. Twelve years ago, freedom was, literally, doing anything I wanted—from posting pictures that were probably a bit inappropriate and yelling at my employees like a stark-raving lunatic, to barking at my clients. These are all things I would never allow myself to do today.

When I decided to be a CrossFit affiliate owner, there were only two rules CrossFit HQ set: have a website and make sure there is a direct link to The CrossFit Journal. Other than that, I could basically do whatever I wanted.

For me to follow the first rule, I had to learn how to make a website. I went online and bought www.albanycrossfit.com on Typepad. This was before there were dozens of CrossFit-specific website creators, which I highly recommend using. I spent entire days—and sometimes weeks—learning how to do everything on this site. It became my life. I was constantly tinkering, adding, finding the latest and greatest widgets for it. At the end of each day, I would have a camera full of at least 200 pictures of the daily workout and upload 12 at a time. This was before smartphones made it simple.

Prior to opening the box, I was relatively structured with my sleep pattern. When I was teaching aerobics class and had to get up at 4 a.m., I'd make sure I was in bed by 10 p.m. But now, with no set structure, I found I was often up past 2 o'clock in the morning. That led me to either getting relatively little sleep and being up at 6 a.m., or foregoing an alarm and sleeping till noon. I was becoming nocturnal.

I was also in a relationship—with the same girl who loaned me $500, which I had proudly paid back by this point. We were living together and I can promise you this: Not going to bed at the same time as your partner on a routine basis does not help your sex life and does not foster a healthy relationship.

I woke up one spring morning to birds chirping and the sun shining and realized the day was half over. It wasn't morning at all. It was past noon. And I had done nothing. Absolutely nothing. Something needed to change.

I had listened to a talk by author and former dot-com business executive Seth Godin. He spoke about having life rules. His three were: no social media, no meetings and no TV. A solid set of rules—for him, not for me. But I ran with it and immediately set rules for myself. After all, no one else was going to do it. I was the inmate running the asylum.

My first set of rules looked like this:

1. Go to bed before midnight.
2. Wake up no later than 9 a.m.
3. Hit the noon class four times per week.
4. Drink a gallon of water every day.

I started small. I believed those four rules wouldn't add too much stress to my life, and they were rules I could implement immediately. That first night was tough. I would typically get home around 9 p.m. By the time I showered, walked the dogs and ate dinner, it was nearly 11 p.m. I forced myself to get the website work done by midnight so I could hit Rule No. 1 By doing that, Rule No. 2 happened seamlessly, which in turn made it easier to be at the noon class. And I showed up with my gallon jug, which I finished by the end of the day.

These rules were a relief. I eventually expanded and adjusted as needed in my life.

Here are some of my current daily rules:

1. My morning routine is not negotiable. I read while using the bathroom, spend 5 minutes meditating, and then I journal.
2. No phone in the bathroom at home. If I'm home and using the bathroom, I'm reading or listening to a book.
3. No more than 2 coffees per day during the week, and no caffeine after 3 p.m.
4. In bed by 11 p.m., up by 7 a.m.
5. Consume a minimum of 1.5 gallons of water.
6. Track my macronutrient intake and consume 800 grams of fruits and vegetables.
7. While driving, listen to something productive: a book or educational podcast.

8. Train. Rest days include a 30-minute minimum of moving. This can be walking, swimming, stretching or Brazilian Jiu-Jitsu.
9. Social media: Keep it to less than 15 minutes.
10. Create a to-do list every evening, review it in the morning, update as needed.
11. Finish working, including spending time on the computer and emailing, by 8 p.m.

Structure gives me freedom. It allows me to live more productively. By following these rules, I have less stress and can be the best version of myself.

Lesson 5

Simple Complex Simple

"I would not give a fig for the simplicity on this side of complexity, but I would give my life for the simplicity on the other side of complexity."
—Oliver Wendell Holmes Jr.

The best athletes make the worst coaches. This isn't always true. But whether you're teaching pull-ups or organic chemistry, I find the more you struggle to learn the topic at hand the better suited you are to teach it.

Matt was the first coach I hired at Albany CrossFit. He walked in one day in a suit, having come from his day job. He had an arrogance about him and rightfully so. This dude was a monster—fit, ripped and good looking. I eyeballed him and encouraged him to do Fran. I was basically hazing him. But I also wanted to see if he was as good as he appeared to be.

As he started to warm-up, Matt told me he was a personal trainer on the side, competed in bodybuilding shows and said he had started to do some CrossFit but wanted to join a real box.

"3, 2, 1, go!"

Matt demolished the thrusters, then hopped on the pull-up bar doing butterfly pull-ups accidentally (this was in 2008, before everyone knew how to do them). He was at the set of 15 in a flash, then wrapped up with unbroken sets of 9 thrusters and 9 pull-ups. The clock read 2:40. This was fucking elite. I was impressed.

Matt then proceeded to lie on the floor for the next two hours while class happened around him. I was a tad concerned, but I knew he would be OK.

Albany CrossFit was growing and this guy was a stud, so I asked him if he would be interested in helping out a bit. He was. Matt got his L1 certificate within a few weeks and started coaching most evenings with me.

One night I noticed him teaching Sam the muscle-up. We only had one set of high gymnastics rings on this contraption we had welded, and the two of them were in the corner for close to an hour. I finally walked over to see what was going on.

"No, just do this," Matt instructed. "Like this. Pull!"

Those were the kinds of cues Matt was giving and Sam was getting frustrated. You see, Matt had muscle-ups on his first attempt. I demonstrated one for him and he proceeded to hop on the rings and do five.

"Like this?"

"Yeah, Matt. Like that."

I, on the other hand, did not have muscle-ups when my first order of rings arrived. I had actually contemplated sending them back as I thought they were defective. I remember getting my first muscle-up as the rings hung from the power rack in the globo gym where I was training. It took me weeks. I was so proud to show it off at my first L1, where Pat Sherwood was teaching.

So, it was no surprise to me that while Matt had no problem getting his first muscle-up, he was struggling to teach it. He never battled through the complexity of a muscle-up like I did—the false grip, pulling to your sternum, the transition, keeping the rings tight.

Matt just grabbed the rings and a second later he was above them.

With most things in life we can look at them in three stages: Simple, complex, simple.

Matt was on the near side (left side) of complexity. He didn't have to battle through it and didn't understand why someone else would.

59

It's the same reason people watch the CrossFit Games and think to themselves, "I can do that." It's because the best in the world make things look easy. You can't see the complexity it took them to get there. It's like an overnight success 25 years in the making.

When you have battled through the complexity of an issue, a movement, a challenge or anything else, you are now on the far side (right side). Muscle-ups are now simple to me because I understand them—I worked through the complexity. And working through the complexity is what allows me to coach them well.

Lesson 6

Fill Your Cup First

"That which we manifest is before us; we are the creators of our own destiny. Be it through intention or ignorance, our successes and our failures have been brought on by none other than ourselves."
—GARTH STEIN

You know how when you get on a plane, the flight attendants tell you to put on your own mask before helping others with theirs? That's for a good reason. You are of no use to anyone else if you die. Morbid, I know. But true. Your wife, child or friend who can't put on a mask definitely can't do it if you didn't put on yours first.

Life is the same.

As business owners, parents, spouses or employees, we often get pulled in so many directions that we are constantly caring for others and neglecting the most important person: ourself.

"Must be so nice to own a gym. You get to work out all day." –every non-gym owner ever.

This couldn't be further from the truth. I cannot begin to tell you the number of times I skipped a day for a business emergency, got stuck on a phone call or was in the middle of my warm-up when a prospective client walked in to the gym.

Thing is, this isn't the right approach. And I realized it one morning in 2011.

My alarm sounded. I woke up and walked into the bathroom, where I saw my reflection in the mirror. I was fat! Not like, "Oh man, I put on a couple of pounds," but legitimately overweight. My eyes welled up.

"How did this happen? I own a freaking gym!" I thought.

It was embarrassing.

In retrospect, I should have seen it coming. I had slowly started wearing baggier shirts, I was skipping more and more workouts, and I had made Ichiban—my favorite Chinese restaurant—No. 2 on my speed dial, only behind my Mom. It was a sad state of affairs.

I had prided myself on living by my "why" and my values. Being healthy is part of both. I was not only unhealthy physically but mentally as well. Working out is my outlet, my passion. It clears my head. But I wasn't doing it. No wonder I wasn't just overweight but depressed.

That moment was all it took. Something had to change. I had to put myself first.

I went online and ordered a barbell, a squat rack and a rower. At the time I owned two gyms and was buying equipment for my house?! That's right. This change had to be big. I realized two things: The later it got in the day, the less likely I was going to work out; and, secondly, now owning two affiliates, I was even busier at the boxes,. After ordering the equipment, I scheduled a daily 6 a.m. WOD on my calendar.

I started that day.

Without having the equipment yet, I still worked out: 100 burpees for time—always a favorite of mine and something you can do anywhere with zero equipment.

Here's the point: Start now! Don't hesitate. If you're waiting for a sign to make a change, THIS IS IT!

By the way, my time was 4:56.

Lesson 7

Be Grateful

"I don't have to chase extraordinary moments to find happiness—it's right in front of me if I'm paying attention and practicing gratitude."
—BRENÉ BROWN

One of the worst things on this entire planet is comparing yourself to others.

Yes, even worse than thrusters.

Comparison is the root of unhappiness. Nothing good comes from it. It sucks so much of our valuable time. We waste it wondering why we are not as good as our neighbors, co-workers or even friends.

When I opened Albany CrossFit in 2007, I was the only box in town. Realistically, not just in town but within about a 50-mile radius. Nowadays, CrossFit affiliates are like Starbucks—some are across the street from one another. In 2007, I could do anything I wanted. I basically had a monopoly on functional fitness. Sure, there were some private studios in town, but no one was having fun like we were.

As CrossFit grew, the CrossFit Games were televised and more people realized they, too, could partake in this fitness revolution. Boxes began opening quickly. While most were owned by former Albany CrossFit coaches and members, some people moved into the area to open an affiliate. Slowly but steadily the Capital Region of New York had over 20 affiliates by 2012.

That's when it happened: Instead of focusing on myself and my gyms, I became more concerned with what others were doing. Worse, I became concerned with how they were doing.

"There couldn't possibly be room for more than one successful box in town," I thought.

For me to do well, that meant others had to do poorly. I now know that's called the "scarcity mindset"—the belief that there is only enough for me.

These days, I am proud to say, I live by the "abundance mentality"—the belief that there is plenty to go around. I've told many box owners that we are not competing with other CrossFit affiliates. There are billions of people on this planet, and they all need to be healthy. There is more than enough to go around. I consider globo-gyms the competition. They offer all the equipment needed to do CrossFit for $9.99/month.

That's where your members will go if you are not providing the value they need.

As these affiliates started opening near mine, I started to have a breakdown. Yet, we weren't losing members to these other affiliates; we were growing. We were the oldest box in the area, had a solid coaching staff, offered the most classes, and were in a prime location for people coming from all directions. I had no reason to stress.

But I did. To the point where it no longer became enjoyable to own my affiliate. And, unfortunately, my behavior had a trickle-down effect. I was making myself so nuts that my coaches not only sensed it but started to feel the same way. They became worried about losing their jobs.

That's when I knew I needed to change my mindset. I set up an appointment with a therapist.

This therapist recommended I start a gratitude journal. I laughed.

"You want me to keep a diary?"

"Well yes, kind of," the therapist replied. "All you have to do every morning is write down three things you are grateful for. If you feel like writing more, great. If not, that's OK, too."

I begrudgingly agreed.

It started off simple: I was grateful for my girlfriend, my dogs, my mom, this cup of coffee. At first, I only felt gratitude in that moment and then I'd go about my day. But after a few weeks, the mindset stayed with me longer and longer. As that was happening, my entries became longer. The practice evolved into me explaining why I was grateful, how it made me feel and how I can show appreciation.

It was at this time that yet another box was opening in town. Another one of my coaches, Chad, was leaving. During my meeting with him, I felt the typical feeling of anger consuming my body as he told me about his dream to own his own affiliate. I took a deep breath and actually felt the anger become joy and happiness.

I realized that here I was, a mediocre trainer who had opened two CrossFit affiliates to incredible success, and I was motivating others to do the same. People were leaving their well-paying jobs to open affiliates because they saw what I had and they too wanted to live the life they loved. Who was I to be mad at that? I should be grateful.

In retrospect, I don't think a boxes only measure of success should be by revenue or total membership but by the number of people you inspire to chase their dreams. The more coaches and members you've inspired to open their own affiliate, to chase their passion, is the true marker for how successful you are as a business owner, coach and leader.

This new-found attitude led me to loaning Chad equipment to get his box up and running, allowing my coaches to help out, and encouraging our membership base to support him and show up for his grand-opening. Changing my mindset actually helped retain our members because they appreciated the support I was giving others, and they felt as if the entire community was growing because of it.

Lesson 8

New Jeans

"Yesterday I was clever, so I wanted to change the world. Today I am wise, so I am changing myself."
—JALAL AD-DIN MUHAMMAD RUMI

I hate shopping for clothes. My mom used to drag me to stores growing up. "Try this on" and "try that on." It was horrific. I am her only child and she enjoyed making sure I looked good and had the trendiest duds. Maybe that's why now, as an adult, I prefer a well worn T-shirt and a pair of jeans to anything else.

To this day, I rarely go clothes shopping. I pride myself on keeping my closet decluttered and prefer to wear the same things over and over again. I have one pair of jeans. So, you can imagine my despair when I threw on my lonely pair of jeans only to find they didn't fit. "Did I shrink them?" was my first thought. Then I remembered I rarely washed them. As much as I wanted to deny it, it was obvious why they didn't fit: I got fat.

69

"You can't outwork a shitty diet" I've said it countless times but at this time I was more of a do what I say, not what I do coach. Although I now had the equipment in my garage and was training regularly I hadn't changed my speed dial just yet.

It was what I refer to as my chubby-affiliate-owner phase—one that is all too common. You open a gym because you love fitness, health and exercise, only to find that you no longer have the time to work out. Instead, you're spending hours on taxes, paperwork and email.

Jeans have never fit me quite right. I have a big butt and thighs, and a small waist. It's not an easy task to find any pants that fit these man curves. I had the perfect pair—not too baggy on the waist or thighs—but now they were too small.

I drove myself to the mall—the last place I wanted to be—and set out to find a new pair. I was trying on so many— too long, too big, too tight. Then finally, like the elusive sub-2-minute Fran, I found them: the right color, style and fit. In a size 34. I had gone from a size 30, bypassed 32 and leapfrogged to 34.

I was embarrassed and ashamed. Here I was coaching CrossFit, preaching nutrition, and I jumped up two pant sizes! I was disgusted with myself.

Head down, I shamefully carried the pants to the register.

"Did you find everything all right?" the cashier loudly asked.

Rocking my new jeans from Relentless, now Edison Atlas.

Did I find everything all right? Did I find everything all right?! No. No, I did not. What I should have found was a brand-new pair of size 30s. No, I shouldn't even be here. My old jeans are fine. I'm the one that's not fine! So, yeah, I found something. But, no, it wasn't all right, dick!

After I had finished my 1-second-long internal monologue, I looked up and smiled.

"Yeah, I did. But you know what? I'm good. I don't actually need them," I politely said.

He didn't give two shits. That's because he didn't realize I had in that moment decided I was going to make a change. I wasn't going to buy those new jeans because I was going to make a change in me. I was going to take control. I would eat better and train more. I would be an example to my community.

It's weird how we can have such memorable and important moments like this in our lives. Moments that will forever stand out and in which you can recall every detail. Those are typically the moments that lead to a profound event in your life. For me this jeans incident was one of the most important events I've ever had.

I went home and immediately began researching flexible dieting. I had recently noticed more and more people posting pictures of donuts and cookies with the hashtag #flexible eating or #iifym (if it fits your macros). That was a diet I could get behind.

From Day 1, I was loving it. Pop tarts? Yes, please. I was eating foods I loved—foods I had been either depriving

My Flexible Eating transformation.

myself of or only eating on so-called "cheat days." No wonder I couldn't lose weight. I was eating thousands upon thousands of extra calories on those cheat days. My typical Saturday often included a pancake breakfast with loads of bacon and sausage, lunch at my favorite pizza spot where I would eat an entire pizza and dinner at Cheesecake Factory where I'd order red velvet cheesecake.

I snacked throughout the day and maybe even took a trip to Five Guys.

Two weeks after I started the flexible diet, the weight started falling off. More and more people were complimenting me on how good I looked. Their comments were often followed by, "What are you doing?" The more that happened, the more I started to think that maybe I could

With Jess Fuller, my first flexible eating client.

Receiving the 40 Under 40 Award with my friends, Jess and Nick.

help people with this nutrition plan. Who wouldn't want to learn how to eat pizza and get lean?

I started with one person: my friend Kayla.

Kayla and I met when she owned this tiny little yoga studio. She recalls that on my first day after my first class I encouraged her to quit her day job as a teacher and dive into business ownership. Ultimately, she did. Now—10 years later—The Hot Yoga Spot is a franchise with more than seven studios.

After our initial conversation, I set Kayla's macronutrient-intake goals. It was about the same caloric intake she was used to but with a different balance of macros—mostly more protein, as Jess was a vegetarian. As she made these changes, her body transformed. She was leaner, her arms were visibly toned, her stomach was flat and she looked 10 years younger. That's when I knew I was on to something.

I started talking to everyone I could about macros. Soon enough, people were seeking me out. I was "The Macro Guy"—the guy eating Cinnamon Toast Crunch and losing weight. And it all started with one seemingly minor decision: Don't buy new jeans.

Lesson 9

Keep the Customer Happy

"Your most unhappy customers are your greatest source of learning."
—Bill Gates

What's the most commonly programmed workout on CrossFit.com?

It's not Fran. Or Murph. It's a 5K run.

So, much to my surprise, every time I programmed a 5K run at my box, no one showed. I don't blame them. I hate running, too. It got to the point where when I needed an "easy" day of coaching, that's exactly what I'd program. It was "3, 2, 1, go! See you all in 30 minutes, and I can chill out."

But one time I programmed the 5K run, it was spring in Albany—my favorite time of the year. The snow had melted, the sun started to shine and it was a beautiful day to hit the road and get on that oxidative pathway.

I was coaching the afternoon classes, and I was anxiously awaiting the arrival of my 3-p.m. athletes. Usually, they would start to roll in around 2:45 p.m. Not today. The 3 p.m. class came and went; no one showed up.

"OK, no biggie," I thought. "I can get some work done."

Then the same thing at the 4 p.m., 5 p.m. and 6 p.m. classes—not one athlete showed up on this beautiful Monday.

While heading home that night, I wasn't sure what to program for Tuesday. Clearly people didn't want to run. But I *knew* they *needed* to run. There was only one solution: I would program the 5K run again for tomorrow. I will get them to run, damn it!

Needless to say, members were not happy. By 10 p.m., I had dozens of texts questioning why I did that, was it a typo, how dare I program the same workout two days in a row. It should be noted: It's not a great idea to give your members your phone number.

I was heated.

I told them in no uncertain terms that they shouldn't question me and that if they didn't like it, there were plenty of gyms in town that were cheaper and would let them do anything they wanted.

In my mind, it was more important to tell these people who were gladly paying me $150 each month that they were dumb. I was smarter, and they could fuck off.

Some of them took me up on that offer. Many, actually. I had created such a strong community that they started a Facebook group and decided amongst themselves to join the globo gym right next door for $9.99/month. By the time I woke up Tuesday morning, I had over a dozen cancelation emails.

Time to check my ego.

While I did want them to run a 5K, I realized my desire to pay my mortgage and keep my heat on was more important than watching people run 3.1 miles—regardless of how beautiful the weather was.

I made one-on-one appointments with every member who had quit and took each of them out to coffee. Turns out they didn't actually want to quit. But I was being an asshole, and they had to teach me a lesson.

It was on one of these coffee meetings with Laura where it finally made sense.

"Jason, we know you know what's best for us. But we pay you, and sometimes you just need to keep us happy."

She was right. I could see this flash before my eyes in so many areas of my life.

Was it really that important for me to show people I was right? Or was it more important to make sure people were happy, having a good time and ultimately coming back?

While a 5K was what they needed, it wasn't what they wanted.

If your goal is to have a successful business or relationship, it's important to remember: It's not about you. It's about everyone else.

Lesson 10

Have Empathy

"When you show deep empathy toward others, their defensive energy goes down, and positive energy replaces it. That's when you can get more creative in solving problems."
—STEPHEN COVEY

Owning an affiliate in 2007 was different than it is today. Most clients walking through the doors back then were what I call "fringe athletes." They were former collegiate athletes, the standard gym member looking for a change or, my favorite, the guy who heard of the CrossFit Games and now planned to win them. The last thing you expected in those days was someone who was clinically obese. Back then, it was unheard of to have a member who had lost more than 100 lbs.

The year was 2008. After a full 365 days had passed, I was surprised to still be in business. Albany CrossFit was thriving. Rarely did a day go by without a new member joining. When I opened, I had hoped for 25 members. In less than a year, I had well over 100.

At Albany CrossFit, we were developing a culture and a strong sense of community. But truth be told, we were all so similar athletically. I had a class for moms in the morning, but everyone else was mostly there to train hard and look better naked.

Enter Jason Murphy.

If you've never seen someone who weighs 500 lbs., the experience is astonishing. There is a stark contrast between someone who is obese and someone who weighs a quarter of a ton. It should be noted: We didn't actually know if Jason

Celebrating at the Albany CrossFit formal with Jason Murphy.

weighed exactly 500 lbs. as many bathroom scale only measure weight up to 400 lbs.

Jason's brother, Josh, referred him to me. Josh was a good friend I met through CrossFit. He had warned me his brother was out of shape and desperately needed to make a change. That warning did not adequately prepare me. Looking back on it, I can't even begin to imagine how intimidating it was for Jason to walk into Albany CrossFit. Many people find it daunting to step inside a CrossFit affiliate. This was Jason's first time ever walking into any gym. Doing so while knowing people would be staring at him must have been overwhelming.

When he arrived, I shook his hand and introduced myself. I had so many thoughts running through my mind: "Where should I start? What should I have him do? Can he even do this?"

One of my coaches, Matt, pulled me aside.

"Bro, he can't do CrossFit. He'll die."

Funny as that statement is now, I know Matt meant it sincerely. Hell, I certainly had my own doubts.

I was scared. But I knew Jason had to do CrossFit or he would, in fact, die.

When you look at someone who is 500 lbs., you don't have to ask them about their nutrition. It's pretty safe to assume it's fucked. My initial thought was to sit him down and spout off the first two sentences of CrossFit's "Fitness in 100 Words:" Eat meats, vegetable, nuts, and seed, some fruit, little starch, and no sugar. Keep intake to levels that support exercise and not body fat.

Had I done that, I'm certain Jason would have shook my hand, said "thanks" and walked out.

It's kind of like drinking out of a fire house. You'll get really wet, but it's not the best way to hydrate yourself. That would have been too much too soon.

The last thing I wanted to do was scare him and regret showing up. I wanted him to change his life. I needed him to come back tomorrow. So, I took him through a workout. It wasn't much. We just reviewed the air squat, did some push-ups on the wall and finished with some rowing. He loved it. He left saying he felt great. We fist bumped and agreed he'd come back tomorrow.

Jason came back the next day and then the next day and the next day after that. He slowly became a fixture in our 9 a.m. class that was mostly filled with women. They loved him. That class played in integral role in his journey; they were the support system he needed. Plus, he had a thing for older women. That helped.

Over that next month, Murph, as we called him, lost 30 lbs. Over the first three months, he lost more than 50 lbs. This was all without changing his nutrition and hitting one workout each morning. Outside of the gym, he continued his normal lifestyle. That included minimal sleep after playing Dungeons & Dragons all night.

As I got to know Jason over those first few months, we became friends. It was hard not to love the guy. He was happy all the time and always brought positive energy to the box. When we would talk about his passion for Dungeons & Dragons, I would bust his balls about the fact that he was living in his parents' basement instead of trying to meet women. I also learned that while playing this game, it was common to consume copious amounts of Mountain Dew. So, one day while chatting with him I made a suggestion.

"Hey, while I don't understand your desire to play this game, what if we just made one small change and instead of regular Mountain Dew, you drank Diet Mountain Dew?"

Jason said he could do that.

That was the first change we made to his nutrition. While it might seem ludicrous to encourage someone to continue drinking soda, we had to start somewhere. Diet Mountain Dew was a step in the right direction. By the next month, Jason had hit the 100-lbs.-weight-loss mark.

As the weeks and months rolled by, we slowly made more tweaks to his diet. The next step was changing the Diet Mountain Dew to water. And while his gaming friends didn't love this change, his body did. As the weight fell off, he inquired more about nutrition.

"What else can I do? What changes should I make next?" he asked me.

I gave him little things to work on: eliminate the potato chips, drink more water, eat one to two pieces of fruit each day. Like a drug dealer, I was trying to get him hooked. The right dose would make him feel amazing and get him jonesing for more. The wrong dose would kill him. Now, I wasn't worried that eating too healthy would actually kill him. I was afraid too much information could stress him out and lead him to stop coming in and making progress.

After getting him to drink more water, the next step I took was to teach him a little about the Paleo diet. This was 2008 and Paleo was all the rage. Murph listened to me for an hour and what he took from that was, "Cool, so I can eat a lot of bacon?" I confirmed as much and that's what he did. I swear I saw him snacking on bacon mid-workout. But it was working. Then we talked about following the Paleo diet all the time. Back then, Murph was a Chef at the local community college. He was quite a good cook, so he came up with some phenomenal Paleo recipes and really took to the lifestyle.

Rather than grabbing fast food on his way home from work, he was preparing his food a week in advance. All the while, he was hitting the 9 a.m. class and making incredible progress. It was around this time that Murph got his first pull-up. His first pull-up! This from the same guy I was worried would have a heart attack on his first day.

"What's next?" he asked.

It was time to introduce the Zone Diet.

I had taken my L1 a few times and was a hardcore believer in the diet, developed by Dr. Barry Sears. I had been following it and saw tremendous success, as did many of our members. I also knew how hard it was.

I taught Murph all about the Zone's block system, and we came up with his first prescription of 20 blocks.

He started immediately and showed up on Day 1 with all of his Tupperware. He was proud. He even told me he was planning on serving Zone-portioned snacks at his next Dungeons & Dragons game. But he was playing that game less often. While Murph was on this journey, he was spending more time hanging out with fellow gym-goers.

Over that next year, Murph made even more changes. He took his L1 course, quit his job, started coaching CrossFit and moved out of his parents' basement.

He also went on dates. Lots of dates. He had spent his whole life hiding from society and avoiding interaction with the opposite sex. Not anymore.

I still remember chatting with him after one of these dates with a woman he had met on match.com. They went out for coffee and it went so well that they went out to dinner afterward, and the date ended with a kiss. A few years later, this woman became his wife.

Murph ultimately got down to 200 lbs. He is now capable of doing just about any CrossFit workout as prescribed, no longer needs medication and is back in school to pursue his dream job of becoming a history teacher.

Now I'm not saying I changed Murph's life, but I changed Murph's life.

But it's only because I had empathy and met him where he was. I made CrossFit the best hour of his day by not overwhelming him and realizing what he was and wasn't ready for.

Empathy is defined as the ability to understand the feelings of another. The more we can do this, the more of an impact we can have on people, both inside and outside of the box.

Stoicism refers to the power of empathy, or the ability to better understand and feel the experiences of another human being. If we can enter the mind of someone else, we can practice and learn a crucial skill, not just for coaching but for life and all of our relationships.

"Acquire the habit of attending carefully to what is being said by another, and of entering, so far as possible, into the mind of the speaker," Marcus Aurelius wrote.

While many of us are frequently waiting for our turn to talk, what if we actually listened and thought about what was being said. It would allow us to better hear and see someone else's emotions. This is the art of listening. Listening is essential for creating an understanding and connecting with others.

Lesson 11

What We Choose to Focus on We Become

"It ain't what you don't know that gets you into trouble.
It's what you know for sure that just ain't so."
—"THE BIG SHORT"

This is the story of our accidental viral video at Albany CrossFit.

Actually, go watch it first. Google Albany CrossFit+Strongman.

In 2011, we decided to do what we called a "weekend revival." It would basically be our own two-day course that would include lectures, multiple workouts, subject-matter experts, a few CrossFit Games athletes teaching and training, and, of course, a wild Halloween party on Saturday night. It went great. Members loved it.

**PR'ing my stone shoulder (just kidding) at
Rob Orlando's first Strongman Seminar.**

Based on the success of the first year, we brought it back again in 2012. Members were excited for it, and we wanted it to be bigger and better.

Our members had really taken a liking to strongman. I had recently taken the inaugural Rob Orlando strongman course, and I quickly filled the box with any and all strongman equipment I could get my hands on: yokes, kegs, stones, logs, tires, you name it. Nothing like lifting heavy shit to clear your head at the end of a stressful day at the office. To my surprise, it was the women who had an affinity for these lifts. As a result, we even formed a strongwoman team that competed and began to make a name for itself.

The head strongman coach, Cat, is now nationally ranked and one of the top lifters in the world. She planned an awesome course for our weekend revival. One portion of the course would cover an odd lift known as the Continental Clean.

The Continental Clean and jerk is not to be confused with the Olympic-lifting-style clean and jerk. While similar, they have notable differences. For one, the Continental Clean uses an axle bar that is thicker and does not spin. It also allows you to rest the bar on your body during the lift. It is truly a functional movement—one you might do at home, if you needed to pick up something heavy to put it on a shelf in the closet.

We had a blast!

Cat taught the lift well. Demoing, explaining, teaching, seeing, correcting—everything she should have done, she did. When it was time for members to lift, they attacked the movement head on. As a coach, one thing that always gets me fired up is seeing women test the boundaries of their strength. To this day, being strong is somewhat frowned up if you're female and, of course, no one wants to "get bulky." But our members did not subscribe to that bullshit and just truly loved lifting heavy shit!

And lift heavy shit, they did.

As was common back then, I'd walk around with my camera and take as many pictures and videos as I could.

When the weekend ended, I posted pictures and videos—one of which would accidentally go down in infamy.

When I posted this particular strongman video on YouTube, it was a pretty standard affair. I typically posted a video every night on our blog. Some spotlighted a member or highlighted the day, others were an interview with an athlete. So, this video went up to little fanfare—other than the people in it really loved watching it.

A little over a week went by. Then, one Tuesday morning, I woke to find my email bombarded with notifications of YouTube comments. I didn't think anything of it at the time. The Albany CrossFit channel usually got its fair share of comments; this wasn't odd. But the comments kept coming. When I finally checked them, I saw they were all bashing our video. And that was the tip of the iceberg. We got emails, phone calls, Yelp reviews, Facebook messages—nearly all of them slamming us for the technique on the clean. We even got a call from CrossFit HQ about it.

Here's the rub: These critics were attacking the lift technique because they didn't know what it was. They thought we had taught an Olympic-lifting-style clean and jerk; they didn't know what a continental clean was. It wasn't until Rob Orlando, himself, posted about it that all the feedback started to slow down. To this day, I still get messages about that video—even though I sold Albany CrossFit over five years ago.

The video was shared, replicated, spoofed and—my all-time favorite—set to circus music! Check that one out.

The point is we see what we want to see. Whether we are right or wrong, we often justify what we see to further our beliefs or judgements.

The athletes in the video were hurt by these comments from people who had no idea what they were talking about. One girl, in particular, Andrea, got a lot of hate. Luckily, she was resilient and didn't give a fuck. Unfortunately, many of us don't realize our words can influence others. Those nasty comments could have caused Andrea to give up strongman or fitness all together—simply because some dummy felt empowered sitting behind a keyboard.

Haters gonna hate.

Cat leading our strongman class.

Lesson 12

Freeze Game

top.

- What are you thinking?
- What are you feeling?
- What are you doing?

Write down the answers to these three questions.

Now, set your alarm for the following times every day: 7 a.m., 9 a.m., 12 p.m., 3 p.m., 7 p.m., or five times that work for your day.

I learned to do this in an effort to become more mindful in my everyday life, as well as to force me to take a deep breath and pause so I can act versus react.

I was watching a new coach of mine teach the push jerk in our on-ramp class for new athletes. As I watched, I noticed a common theme amongst these 12 athletes: Not one of them was opening their hips. Not one.

The first point of performance of the push jerk is hip extension. If you're not using your hips, you're blunting your potential power output.

I lost my mind. How could this happen? How could this coach not notice this? I immediately ran to the group and took over. I must have looked like a lunatic, running around while saying "squeeze your butt," "jump harder," "hit your head to the ceiling," and any other cue I could pull from my arsenal.

It wasn't just a bad impression, it was bad coaching. I let my emotions get the better of me. Rather than taking a step back and approaching this in a tactful manner, I had a knee-jerk reaction. I wound up fixing no one.

After this fiasco, the coach approached me. He was upset and rightfully so. He was mad. I was frustrated, I talked to him about hip extension and, ultimately, I apologized. We also set up a time for him to work with me on coaching the push jerk. I learned some lessons along the way.

First: Don't just come up with problems, have solutions. I did solve the problem of his push-jerk coaching, but that wasn't a solution to my overreacting. I merely put a Band-Aid on it by apologizing.

In time, as I learned of the Freeze Game and started to try and implement it in my life I did solve this problem. It

Coaching a class at CrossFit Soulshine.

wasn't overnight. I started the same way I recommend, but simply plugging in alarms throughout the day that would remind me to take a moment. I started a note on my phone to write them down as I was more likely to do it on my phone, seeing as how I had to shut the alarm anyway.

At first, they were vague and shallow.

Q: What are you thinking?

A: About the Freeze Game.

Q: What are you feeling?

A: Happy.

Q: What are you doing?

A: Typing this.

That was ok, more importantly it made me pause and reflect, even if just a few seconds. But the more I did them and the longer, the better I got at them, the more I enjoyed them, and the more I got out of them. Suddenly, I was becoming more aware of everything I was doing, focusing more on each moment, and most importantly able to prevent reacting.

The trigger became any time I was going to change or raise my voice. It was my cue to take a deep breath and ask myself the three questions. It's not only that by thinking of the answers it helped me gain a new perspective, but it was also the fact that I had to pause before speaking.

This is a tactic I still use to this day. There are plenty of times Roz and I are in a heated debate and I will just take a deep breath and pause, she knows exactly what I'm doing, but it works every time.

Lesson 13

Know Your Value

"Price is what you pay, value is what you get."
—WARREN BUFFETT

I opened Albany CrossFit in 2007. This was before the plethora of membership software and operating systems became available to box owners.

When someone joined the box, they had two options for payment: cash or check. About a year later, I got fancy and offered PayPal. I kept track of everyone in a notebook and had to chase people down to collect their monthly dues. It was inefficient. I had to chase after people, wait for them to write a check or rummage through their pockets for cash. I also had to make daily trips to the bank to make deposits.

My opening rate was $50/month. I was nervous as hell! Would people actually pay $50 each month to train with me? They could join any standard gym for about $10 a month. Why would they pay five times more than that to train in my dirty gym, where most of the equipment came from craigslist?

Every time a new person walked in, I became anxious to discuss rates. I would look away, afraid to make eye contact, try to avoid the topic as long as possible. But, inevitably, it would come up: How much? Even though I would freak out a little every time cost came up, people kept signing up. It was when I had reached about 100 members that I finally gained confidence in what I was charging. That's when I decided to increase the price.

Uh oh.

Just thinking about it made me uneasy.

How many members would we lose?

Everyone is going to complain.

I spent hours crafting the perfect email to send, explaining in excruciating detail how we would use the money from this price increase to do so many amazing things: more classes, new equipment, hiring a staff.

I was embarrassed to even consider taking more money for me. Was I running a nonprofit? Should I feel guilty for wanting to make more money? Hell no!

I sent the email with trepidation, anxiously awaiting a swarm of negative responses. They never came.

As I got to the box the next day, I was sure everyone would be waiting with pitchforks to crucify me. At the time, it was a substantial increase. Double, to be exact. Although

$50 was an expensive globo-gym membership, it was far below the CrossFit-affiliate standard. I knew I wouldn't be able to afford new equipment or hire coaches without substantially more money coming in.

When I first opened, the average box was charging about $120 a month. Yet, something in my head kept telling me, "That's too much" and "you can't ask for that." So, I settled on $50. I de-valued myself. I didn't think I was good enough to charge the industry standard and, a year later, the gym was full.

Now that it was time to increase the rate, I had to wrap my head around another lesson: It's OK to make money. Money isn't evil. Just because I was in the service industry didn't mean I should be afraid to get paid. Get that cheddar!

Members, unfortunately, often do "box math."

It goes something like this: "There are 100 members and Jason is charging $100 per person. He's making millions! He's greedy!"

But why don't I deserve that? I was busting my butt, pouring everything I had into the gym. It was my baby. It was OK to cut myself a check.

There was some backlash, but it was nothing like what I was building up in my mind. At the end of the day, we didn't even lose a single member. That's right: 100 percent of our athletes stayed, and I doubled our gross income with one email.

If you bring value, members will appreciate it and be willing to pay whatever you ask.

Lesson 14

Do Less Better

"If you don't prioritize your life, someone else will."
—Greg McKeown

Focus.

Let me give you a broad-brush overview: Focus on what's essential in your life, your business and your relationships. When you concentrate on the truly important things, you do them well rather than being pulled in a million directions only to do nothing well.

When I opened Albany CrossFit, the schedule was all over the place. Monday's schedule was different from Tuesday's, which was different than Wednesday's because each day was based around my personal life. I was still teaching and training others, so I had to accommodate my existing schedule.

The only classes listed online or on the fancy pamphlet I created were "WOD." That's literally all it said. After all, that's all we did: CrossFit.

As membership grew and my finances got a bit more comfortable, I slowly started to change my personal schedule. If you were a one-on-one client, I encouraged you to join the box and do CrossFit. I also ended teaching obligations that didn't benefit the box. That was a life lesson in itself: If I had time to work, it should be for my business—not for someone else's. While that quick money and paycheck might have been more than I made that hour working for myself, it didn't feel right. I realized that while I might not be able to quantify the hour spent working on my business, if I truly wanted to grow that hour was more valuable spent working for myself.

As I gave up these other obligations, the schedule got more streamlined. Weekday classes happened at 5 a.m, 6 a.m., 7 a.m., 9 a.m., 12 p.m., 3 p.m., 4 p.m., 5 p.m., 6 p.m., 7 p.m., 8:30 p.m. Yup, 11 classes. Weekends were less busy with three classes each morning and an afternoon class on Saturdays.

Even with all of those classes, I felt the need to add more. I wanted to add more specialty options. I chased after every seminar I could: weightlifting, rowing, striking, gymnastics, kettlebells. I was thirsty for knowledge and wanted to pass it on to our members. Our schedule doubled and then tripled. Every hour had multiple options. You could hit the daily CrossFit workout, do a gymnastics class or even a yoga class. Members were loving it.

Every time we would offer a new class, they would be jam packed. Likewise, we often had to cap attendance.

Here's what I noticed:

Week 1 was full.

Week 2 was busy.

Weeks 3 and 4 only included a handful of people.

Here I was paying for more coaches, stretching the schedule thin, and members weren't even taking the classes. Although they were pumped Week 1, by Week 3 they just wanted to get back to regular classes.

It wasn't about the money or the fact that we were offering something really incredible. It was confusion. Why weren't more people hopping into these awesome options?

It was then I realized the issue: They joined to do CrossFit. That's what they loved.

While they could still get the community, the whiteboard and the PRs in the specialty classes, it just wasn't the same.

These specialty classes weren't essential. I was distracting them from what they loved. And, I could implement portions of these classes within the WOD, giving them the best of both worlds. Plus, I would save a bunch of time and money, and my coaching staff would be significantly less stressed.

*

With Josh Murphy and Kate Foster celebrating CrossFit for Hope.

In 2011, CrossFit HQ launched the charity event CrossFit for Hope to benefit St. Jude Children's Research Hospital in Memphis, Tennessee. Albany CrossFit made it our goal to raise the most money of any affiliate. We did that by collecting over $100,000. We went on to do it again in 2012. Both years, CrossFit HQ flew me to Memphis to receive the affiliate award for most money raised. I'm very proud of that.

Like most things I've achieved, this was the result of many people's hard work and effort. Our community was strong. Had you asked members why they belonged to Albany CrossFit, I'm sure many would answer "Because it's a family." Few would say, "Because of the workouts."

Based on the success of this fundraiser and how much fun everyone seemed to have at the party, it was my bright idea to do more. If one party was good, one per month would be even better. In 2012, we hosted a party every month. Each one had its very own theme. We repeated our talent-show fundraiser and added game nights, a Halloween party, a winter holiday party, quiz night and a potluck, to name a few. Basically, as soon as one party was over, we had a meeting to start organizing the next one.

While members appreciated the effort, we noticed it was always the same 20 or so athletes that came to every party. They were our best members. Although it was important to keep them happy, we were spending a lot of time and money on these parties. Only one party every quarter was well attended; the rest were lackluster.

After that year, we realized we were trying to do too much. Our community didn't need 12 parties every year to keep it strong. One amazing party would be better than 12 subpar get-togethers.

Accepting an award at St. Jude's Childrens Research Hospital.

That's when we made the switch to a formal. Imagine your high-school prom but with an open bar, no chaperones and awards. We went all out: rented a hotel, full catering, open bar, black tie, you name it.

And we created some amazing awards: Member of the Year, Rookie of the Year, Outstanding Member of the Community, Most Improved and even a Hall of Fame for some of our most tenured athletes. The community loved it. While in the past we would get 20 to a busy party, we had over 90 percent of our members sign up to come. Many brought their significant others who weren't members. It exceeded our expectations and became an annual tradition everyone eagerly anticipated.

It's not about doing *all* the things but doing fewer things better.

Lesson 15

Be Patiently Impatient

"When someone is impatient and says, 'I haven't got all day,' I always wonder, 'How can that be? How can you not have all day?'"
—GEORGE CARLIN

Owning a business leads you down many paths. When I first opened, I knew about coaching people.

Over the years, I developed other skills:

- How to create and update a website
- Photography
- Video editing
- How to build gym equipment
- Microsoft Excel
- Public speaking

One thing I never mastered was craftsmanship. It never came easy, and I realized it took me much longer than it was worth. Eventually I decided to hire someone. It felt great. Here I was successful enough to pay someone to do something I didn't want to.

I found a handyman.

The first project I gave him was fairly simple: a new front desk. I had been operating this business from my high-school desk. It was time for an upgrade. The handyman jumped at the opportunity and delivered. He did so well I recommended him to quite a few people, and his business started to grow.

When it came time for our next project, I was excited to call him up again. I wanted storage for all of our wall balls. We had over 40 at this point, and they were piled in the corner. I needed the floor space. He stopped by, drafted some designs and got to work. I noticed this time things went a bit slower. Rather than starting the project and working on it until it was complete, he wouldn't even come in every day. The project wound up taking more than twice as long as he originally quoted. But it was all good—it looked nice, and the members were thrilled with the new-found floor space we turned into a mobility area.

Then it came time for a huge project: I wanted to expand the gym. We had grown and while we were already occupying

Major expansion at Albany CrossFit.

more space, it was divided by a 20-foot concrete wall. We were in adjacent racquetball courts; I wanted to make it one big area. Once again, I called up the same handyman and explained the scope of the project. He knew it would be big but let me know he could definitely handle it and was ready to get started.

The project began on a Saturday. The goal was to be done by week's end. The timeline was important because while he removed the wall, we were running classes outdoors.

Things started great. Brick by brick, the wall was coming down. But then, three days in, he didn't show up. The next day, the same thing happened. I called him, furious.

"Where are you? What's going on? It's supposed to rain next week. We need this done!"

He explained he had taken on other projects and was being stretched thin, so mine was going to take a bit longer than anticipated.

I was mad, but I listened. I reiterated just how important it was for the project to be done on time. He promised it would be and to be in the next day to get it finished by early the next week.

He did come in the next day, but that was it. He missed the following day again.

I fired him immediately.

He had become my friend over the years, but that was it. I gave him a chance and he didn't live up to expectations.

My coaches freaked out. My members weren't happy. So, I had no choice.

This is how owning a gym taught me to use a jackhammer, a forklift and how to knock down a concrete wall. It also taught me that you need municipal approval before making structural changes to a building.

Remember, it can be a slow journey. Have patience but keep moving forward.

Lesson 16

Tough Love is Still Love

"Being entirely honest with oneself is a good exercise."
—Sigmund Freud

At the same time as CrossFit was gaining steam, so was mixed martial arts (MMA).

Many of the local fighters started training at Albany CrossFit. It was during that time that Andy, who fought in the pre-UFC days, started training with us.

Super tough guy, intimidating as hell, tattooed before it was cool and so funny. But

Andy was more than just a monster. He was a solid member of the community. He had a family with young children and didn't come to many social events. But in classes, Andy was the first one done and the first one cheering everyone on, helping out when needed and always welcoming to new members.

Andy truly represented what Albany CrossFit was all about. So, it was a surprise and disappointment when I saw that change. Andy went from being someone who enjoyed class and was happy with everything we did, to complaining about everything we did.

In 2008, Albany CrossFit was basically "Animal House." We worked out hard and partied harder. At one such party, a couple people had a few too many beverages, got drunk and might have done Fran. I might have been one of those people. This also might have occurred stripped down to our underwear. This was before everyone had smartphones. Still, it was documented through pictures and videos. A good time was had by all. No harm done except we might have vomited afterward and been very hungover the next day.

Andy came in on Monday, angered that we would do this. I pointed him to such videos as "In n Out Fran" and other CrossFit shenanigans, and I explained it was just a bunch of young people letting off steam. In retrospect, I think jealousy might have played a role. He had been at home that night, unable to enjoy the party with his friends.

But that was just the tip of the iceberg.

What really started to infuriate me was how Andy decided he had to make every workout a little bit "harder" than prescribed. In other words: "Hey, I'm going to go with

135 lbs. instead of 95 lbs." Or, "I'm going to do chest-to-bar pull-ups instead of regular pull-ups."

I put "harder" in quotes because while that might look harder on paper, any experienced CrossFitter knows it's easier. By going heavier, he was adding more rest. Turns out there's not much intensity when you're staring at a bar instead of moving it.

Plus, like I said, he just became ornery and generally unpleasant to be around. He would complain about other people, complain about their movement, their reps, their range of motion, everything. At the same time, it was also obvious that Andy was no longer the big dog at the box. When he first joined, he was the best. He was a badass. He would regularly record the best time of the day. He came from an athletic background, was a former mixed martial artist and embraced hard work. He was not afraid of going into that pain cave. But as CrossFit grew, he was getting outranked.

Then, other members started asking if they could—or should—be lifting more weight "like Andy does." That was the last straw.

It was time for Andy and and I to chat.

I knew it would be a tough conversation. But I wanted to get to the roots of the problem rather than remaining frustrated every time he came in. I talked to him about intensity, one of my favorite topics. I explained force multiplied by distance and then divided by time equals intensity. I also explained that by changing every workout, he was basically saying our programming was shit. Plus, he was robbing himself of results. He wasn't getting the intensity he needed, I told him. Intensity is where the magic happens. As Coach Glassman said, "Intensity is the independent variable most commonly associated with maximizing favorable adaptation to exercise." In simple terms: Intensity equals results.

I explained all of this to him and also that as a member of our community, it was important to me that he did the same workouts as everyone else. People looked up to him.

"Andy, I'm trying to help you. I'm trying to help you get results, and you're not listening to me. This is something I know a lot about. This is something I'm educated in and, again, this is my business, and I'd like for you to do it this way."

He was not having it. He got defensive and angry, said he pays for his membership and his changing the workout wasn't a big deal. If he wants to go heavier, it was his business.

I promptly fired him. That's right: I looked him dead in the eyes and said while I appreciate the time he spent with us, if that was his attitude he was no longer welcome as a member of Albany CrossFit. Not gonna lie: It felt a-mazing!

At this point, I'd been training people for 15 years. Some wretched people, some annoying, some smelly, but no matter what, I took their money and kept on training them.

This was liberating.

"I don't need or want your money. I am trying to grow a community and my business. Your money is no longer good here!"

To say he was taken aback was an understatement. He was furious. For a moment, I was scared he was going to kick my ass. Instead, he stormed out of the office. I knew I'd made the right decision. Too often, we let people do things they think is best, when, in reality, we know what is best and are too gentle in our delivery so the message doesn't get through. Sometimes it takes being real, putting our foot down and knowing that this kick in the ass you are giving them is actually just what they need.

Turns out it was exactly what Andy needed.

After a few weeks, he showed up at the box. He pulled me aside and asked if we could chat. We, once again, went to my office. But this time, he was singing a different tune.

He started by apologizing and saying I was right. Andy admitted he had been changing the loading because he was embarrassed he was no longer the the gym's top performer; it was an excuse to explain his lower ranking on the leaderboard.

Andy went on to say that firing him opened his eyes. Although he was angry at first, he later realized I was spot on. That became glaringly apparent to him when he did Albany CrossFit workouts at a globo gym and realized how much harder they were as written versus with heavier weights or higher-skill gymnastics movements.

The conversation ended with a handshake and maybe even a man hug. I'm proud to say Andy is still hitting CrossFit workouts as prescribed to this day and once in a while still finds himself on top of the leaderboard.

Lesson 17

Wanting vs. Deciding

"It is not the man who has too little, but the man who craves more, that is poor."
—Seneca the Younger

When I found CrossFit in 2006, affiliates weren't common. Instead, you interacted with fellow CrossFitters via an online forum CrossFit HQ managed. I made a lot of friends through this forum and happened to find the one other guy in upstate New York who did CrossFit and invited him to the Plyometrics class I taught at the globo gym. It was basically "CrossFit light."

Like me, Brett was doing CrossFit in his garage. Coming to a gym to work out with other people who were also trying to get fit was a first for him. We hit it off well and he started coming to this class regularly. Although I would only be teaching it a few more weeks as I got ready to open my first box.

Brett hitting some heavy Overhead Squats.

I met Brett at exactly the right time as he wanted to coach CrossFit. He had a "real job," a wife and two kids, which made it tough for him to coach any time outside of 5 a.m. That worked great for me because I hated getting up early. From Day 1, I had my 5-a.m. class covered. Pretty sweet!

From the beginning, Brett was upfront about his plans to one day open an affiliate. I appreciated his transparency and knew he wanted to open a box about 20 minutes from mine. I wasn't particularly concerned.

From the start, Brett would regularly change the workouts, modify the warm-ups, run classes long,—basically do anything he wanted with the 5 a.m. class. I was to blame. I let him do it and rarely showed up at that time, so he knew he could get away with it. I was still new at being a business owner and a boss and was not prepared to deal with insubordination. Plus, Brett was different. If I had to describe him in one word, I'd say "unique" only because "weird" is pejorative. "Quirky" might be better. Brett was a creature of habit, set in his ways and liked to do things the way he liked to do them. The 5 a.m. class seemed to exist on an island. Still, he showed up regularly and on-time, and did a great job coaching the appropriately dubbed "Morning Mayhem" bunch.

Over time, Brett and I ended up butting heads often. And he would frequently retort with "When I open my box" and "This is how I'll do it when I open."

At this point, Brett had been coaching at Albany CrossFit for over two years. During one particularly heated argument, I finally yelled, "Then fucking do it!"

I get it: He had a real job, a wife, two kids. It wouldn't be easy for him to open a small business. But stop telling me about how you're going to do things when you finally open. Stop telling me about how great your make-believe box will be. Stop talking and start doing.

Don't get me wrong: I didn't want him to leave. But I was sick of his comments.

During this blow-up, I calmed down and continued with, "Enough is enough. Either you need to do things my way, stop treating this like it's your own gym or finally go and actually open your own box."

As Brett was known to do, he stared at me awkwardly.

Finally, he laughed, which somewhat broke the tension but also made me feel like he was going to stab me and wear my face as a mask.

His laugh was his realization that while he really wanted to open a box, he knew it would probably never happen. His wife wasn't onboard with quitting his well-paying job to "play CrossFit," as she put it. Having never been married at that point, I pretended to understand.

We sat there for a while and discussed what he liked and what he'd change. Rather than continuing to argue, we both made compromises. I let him take over the programming, for example, so all classes would do the same workout. In return, he agreed to take on one evening class each week to be more involved with the community.

I don't blame Brett for his decision. Now being married, I understand the importance of your spouse's support and making sure you're doing what's best for the family. So many people are in similar situations. They want to lose weight, find their soulmate or make more money.

Wanting is easy—anyone can do that. Deciding is the hard part. But when you actually decide to do something and set your mind to it—and know nothing will stop you from accomplishing this goal—that's when change begins.

Lesson 18

Smarter Not Harder

"Be impressed by intensity, not volume."
—GREG GLASSMAN

One of the reasons many people fall in love with CrossFit is because of its potency.

In less than an hour, you can get your ass appropriately handed to you and get really fucking fit along the way. Before finding CrossFit, many of us spent countless hours at the gym on movements that isolated muscle groups and on cardio that allegedly put us in the "fat-burning zone."

But despite its potent dose in little time, some still hanker for more.

"If this much training got me good, it only makes sense that more training will get me even better," seems to be the prevailing thought.

We then seek out the latest and greatest programming out there. Maybe it's CompTrain or CrossFit Invictus or Misfit Athletics.

Coaching during a L1 seminar.

No doubt they are all good and they serve a purpose. But what purpose and for whom?

The CrossFit Games are unique in that the average Joe gets to compete against the best in the world in the annual Open. As a result, many people believe they need to train they way elite athletes do. But consider this: The best of the best train for a living. They don't work a 9-5 job, they have their food prepared for them and they get plenty of rest and relaxation. Training is their job.

The average Joe crams training into an already-busy day.

It would be akin to me training mixed martial arts as a hobby and then wanting to step into the octagon with Conor McGregor. Not a good idea.

So, we fall in love with CrossFit because it fits our busy day. But then it actually makes our days busier and gives us less time to do the things we love, such as enjoying hobbies, spending time with family or going on a date.

The average—hell, even the above-average CrossFitter—does not need more. They need better. When we hit more than one workout a day, one of them inevitably gets half-assed.

In 13 years of doing CrossFit, I have seen this happen so often I had a tough time choosing which example to use. Ultimately, I settled on Kevin.

I chose Kevin because he truly was a badass athlete. An athlete who actually warranted additional training.

When Kevin joined Albany CrossFit, he was still in school wrapping up his nursing degree. He loved CrossFit because of its efficiency. He'd come to class, hit the workout, often record a top score and then go back to school.

After graduation, he had way more time on his hands. So, inevitably that led him to spend more time at the box. He was there so often, at one point I asked him if he was sleeping there.

Here's the rub: While Kevin was making improvements in his overall performance, I made two observations:

1. The improvements he was making were not worth the time he was training. Sure, his lifts were getting heavier and his times faster, but the weights were only fractionally heavier and the times only mere seconds faster. Meanwhile, he was spending hours upon hours at the gym. It was the law of diminishing returns.

2. Perhaps even more importantly, he was no longer having fun. Originally, CrossFit was his stress relief and social outlet. Now it was his job. I could see it in his demeanor. He was no longer excited when he arrived. Instead, he resembled an office worker punching in for another day at his boring desk job.

Whenever someone approaches me about doing more training or getting personal programming, I do two things:

1. I ask them about their nutrition. If you don't have a solid nutrition foundation, you don't deserve the right to do more. It's like building a house and worrying about the size of your attic when you don't have any concrete laid.

2. I make them do squat therapy. Squat therapy is the most beneficial addition you can do for your training. Your squat

is a window into your overall movement. If you can't squat well, you are functioning at a fraction of your potential. Before worrying about doing more, you have to move better. You have to earn it. I have seen squat therapy take people to their next level way faster and safer than adding more volume, and it takes a fraction of the time.

Most people who want to train more just need to move better and get another hobby.

Lesson 19

How You Do One Thing is How You Do Everything

"Before enlightenment, chop wood, carry water.
After enlightenment, chop wood, carry water."

—ZEN PROVERB

CrossFit affiliates are like the "The Real World" of the fitness community. Each one has the same characters:

- The woman who doesn't like to lift heavy for fear of getting bulky.
- The dude who always wants to go heavier because, as we all know, it's easier.
- The person that's always 5 minutes late to class.
- The guy that uses too much chalk.

- The beast.
- The member that always does "abs" after every class.
- And, of course, the rep shaver.

Ah, the rep shaver.

We all know this person. This person is, indeed, improving, but, all of a sudden, posts a few suspicious scores. So, one day you decide to count this person's reps. Lo and behold, this person missed a few. Maybe this person was "WOD drunk" and this was just a fluke. But it happens again on the next workout, and the next. And all of a sudden you're consumed with this person's violation. You're actually spending more time worrying about this person's scores than your own. Sound familiar?

We spend so much time worrying, getting mad, complaining and, of course, gossiping about this person. And, really, why? What's the point? What are we trying to get out of this?

In over a decade in the CrossFit world, I have had way too many conversations about someone who's cheating a workout. I'm always dumbfounded. As I'm listening to this person complain, I'm wondering, "Why do you care so much? What impact does this have on your performance or any aspect of your life?"

Often in life, we become concerned with things outside our control that have no direct impact on our lives. No different than being mad at the traffic you're sitting in, the plane that's delayed or Chipotle for being out of queso. Ain't nothin' you can do about it! Accept it and move on. Someone cheating at CrossFit is no different.

Let me tell you about Bill.

Bill joined Albany CrossFit and everyone loved him. Eager to learn, he gave 100 percent at every class. Slowly but surely, he made his way up the leaderboard. Truthfully, maybe a bit too fast. He became the talk of the box—and not in a good way.

Every class he was in, a group of athletes would gather around him in an effort to "cheer him on." In reality, they were counting his reps. It was a cancer at the box.

They would watch and mock him, talking amongst themselves about how he was shaving reps—all behind his back, of course. To his face, they would congratulate him and give him high-fives. It all culminated during the workout Isabel, a classic of 30 snatches at 135 lbs. A really good time is sub-3 minutes. Bill did it in 2:12—an obscenely fast time, especially considering he was still relatively new to CrossFit.

Turns out one of our members had secretly recorded Bill's effort. He did 18 reps—60 percent of the work. I was sick of it. I was frustrated that Bill was cheating and even more frustrated that people cared so much. I've always felt that if someone was cheating at CrossFit, there were more

131

underlying issues than I cared to deal with—even with my master's degree in psychology.

I asked Bill to chat with me in my office.

It was so awkward. Ever have to accuse a grown man of cheating at exercise? Of course, he denied it. That's when I pulled out the video of him doing 18 reps. Embarrassed was an understatement. There were tears. Yes, a grown-ass man was crying about cheating at fitness.

Outside of the gym, Bill was a husband, he had a child, a good job as a sales rep and was genuinely a nice person. He would help out whenever needed at the box, socialized with all the members and had even expressed an interest in coaching.

Point is, I know he wasn't a "cheater" in real life, but I told him he was getting a bad reputation around the box and many people were talking behind his back. While I understood his desire to be viewed as a top athlete, he was actually achieving the opposite effect. He was getting talked about often, but not in the way he envisioned.

People assumed that because he cheated on his workouts, he cheated in life. He was labeled "a cheater." People assumed he cheated at work, on his wife, anywhere he could.

"Is that the reputation you want?" I asked him.

"No need to apologize to me or the members. I just want you to come back tomorrow and do everything here the way you do outside of here—with integrity."

And he did.

The next day, Bill was no longer at the top of the leaderboard. He was somewhere near the middle. No one noticed or cared. And that's where he stayed for quite some time. Slowly and steadily, he worked his way up that leaderboard one rep, one workout at a time.

About six months later, we programmed Isabel again. He approached me prior to the class and told me how excited he was to do this "legit" this time. Legit, he did, as he crushed his previous time and was the fastest of the day at 1:47. It was recorded again, but this time for him, and he was exceedingly proud of what he'd accomplished.

After class, Bill pulled me aside and thanked me for the talk I had with him six months earlier. He told me he had been so embarrassed he had contemplated leaving the box—even quitting CrossFit—but my words kept running through his mind. He wanted to show everyone the type of person he was.

Lesson 20

Choose Your Company Wisely

"Associate with those who will make a better man of you."
—Seneca the Younger

If you've ever been crabbing, you know you can leave crabs in a bucket without the risk of losing any. You don't even need a very deep bucket. Here's why: As a crab is close to making its escape, one of its buddies grabs it with its claws to pull it back down. Breakout thwarted. Destiny: someone's delicious fried-crab dinner.

Now, take that same story and apply it to your life. Are your friends the kind who pull you back into the bucket? Or do they offer their shoulders for escape?

One of my favorite group of women that I had at the box was my "moms in training" bunch. They were six women who joined together. They hired a babysitter to come along, so they could ensure their kids were in good hands while they trained. How that poor girl watched 13 kids for that hour is beyond me. But none of them died, so I assume she did her job well.

Those moms came in 3 days per week at 8 a.m. after dropping off older kids at school or helping them get on the bus. They loved CrossFit as their one hour away from parenting.

Laura, Annie, Kimi, Sue, Roxanne and Nancy. They became great friends and all of them still do CrossFit to this day.

When they first joined, they were all out of shape. Some of them had athletic experience, Roxanne even being a former collegiate athlete. But mothers and matriarchs of their families didn't give them a lot of alone time; they all let health slide down on that list of priorities. In the beginning, they were deconditioned. They were also ecstatic to have time away from their kids. So, they spent most of their time chatting and laughing, which was fine by me. I was glad to see them happy, and they always got their workout in—there was just more giggling than chalk.

As the months rolled by, these women accidentally got fitter. I say "accidentally" because they were really at the box to have a good time; fitness was a byproduct. As in most groups, one of them really stood out. In this case, it was Laura.

Laura was the first to do most things: the first to get a pull-up, the first to deadlift 300 lbs., the first to do a handstand push-up, the first to do Fran Rx. She was really becoming a stellar athlete. Laura was ready to level up. But her friends were pulling her back in the bucket.

They weren't being malicious like the crabs; they just didn't understand how important this had become to Laura. Being the nice person she was, Laura was concerned about hurting other people's feelings.

Laura and I discussed this, and we came up with a solid game plan. She would start coming to our 5 a.m. class before any of her kids went to school. This eliminated the need for a sitter when she was in class.

Laura quickly became an integral member of that Morning Mayhem class, and her fitness level skyrocketed.

Laura Mirkovic long-time member and close friend.

The Morning Mayhem class included a different breed of athletes. Anyone who gets up at 4 a.m. to work out is a little crazy and clearly very motivated. Laura was given the challenge of either stepping up or stepping out; she chose the former.

Laura's fitness level increased so dramatically, she placed in the Top 20 at that year's CrossFit Games North East Sectional in Albany. It was an amazing feat given that less than one year earlier she had her third child.

Often times we are just so accustomed to the people we hang out with that we don't take the time to stop and think about the impact they're having on us mentally, emotionally and physically.

While Laura remained friends with those moms, she knew that in order to hit her goals at the box she would need to surround herself with new friends.

Lesson 21

Argue Like You're Right, Listen Like You're Wrong

"Well, I ain't always right, but I've never been wrong."
—THE GRATEFUL DEAD

You can never be certain.

We go through life assuming we're right in our behaviors, our thoughts, our actions. It was easy for me to think I was always right—I was the boss. Although I'd get feedback, criticism and ideas thrown at me, ultimately, I was the decision maker. And when your business is growing in no small part thanks to the dozens of decisions you make on a daily basis, you begin to believe you're always right. That's a mistake.

"It is the mark of an educated mind to be able to entertain a thought without accepting it," Aristotle wrote.

To me, that means we can all see the same thing but interpret it in different ways.

How often do we ask ourselves, "What if I'm wrong?" And perhaps more importantly, "What would it mean if I were wrong?"

I can tell you that while I owned three boxes, it was rare that I asked myself these questions. Now, years removed, I do this daily. I've learned for change to happen in my life, I must be wrong about something. Think about it: If you're existing but unhappy every day, you're already wrong about something significant in your life. Until you're able to figure it out, nothing will change. That's not to say you can't ever be right, but don't be dumb like I was and assume you always are.

My decision to open a second box was a tough one. I wanted to grow my business but also help get more people find CrossFit. I had brought on six full-time coaches, over 20 assistant coaches, four interns and even a front-desk employee. I was ready to take it to the next level.

Albany CrossFit was booming, classes were packed, we had over 500 members. Still, I was nervous. I had doubt. Was this a fluke? Would I be a one-hit wonder? I started thinking it would be a whole lot easier to stay here and avoid exploring options for a second box. As with most issues, I discussed it with my coaching staff. Could they even handle another place to coach?

At the Albany CrossFit formal with Caleb.

That's when one of my coaches stepped up. Not only did Caleb encourage me to open another location, he said he wanted to be part of it. Mind you, Caleb and I were besties, inseparable since the day he asked to be an intern. Work for me for free? Of course, you can. Welcome to the team!

We hit it off and, before long, he was coaching classes and was added to the payroll. What was supposed to be a quick three-month internship turned into his first full-time job. Members absolutely loved him. It was hard not to. He had a young energy and a killer six pack that he wasn't afraid to flaunt. The ladies adored him.

We spent most of our days together, training, goofing around. To say I favored him over my other coaches would be a major understatement. We rarely argued and that was mostly because any time our opinions differed, I quickly shot him down. Caleb never spoke up because he was trying to be respectful.

Finding the balance between being best friends and colleagues was tough. Like the time he wasn't doing a very good job maintaining the website. Rather than getting to the root of the problem by simply asking why, I doubled down. I told him that now he was not only responsible for posting the WODs but also creating blog content. Hey, I was new to being a boss.

I still remember the excitement of driving back to Albany CrossFit after we signed the lease in Clifton Park for the second space. Clifton Park was about 20 miles north, far enough away that we would attract new members, but close enough that members could use both spots and we could have joint functions.

If Albany CrossFit was done on a shoestring budget, CrossFit Clifton Park was the polar opposite. No expense was spared: brand-new equipment, TVs, a decked-out office, a fabricated pull-up rig. Getting the doors open cost well over six figures. The challenge was while I was fronting the majority of the money, Caleb was doing most of the work. This was to be his project and baby. I would continue to oversee Albany CrossFit while he took on the new, shinier box.

There was so much grey area in this.

Albany CrossFit assumed the father-figure role. Anything and everything that could be shared, Albany CrossFit paid for: member software, websites, music, coaching development.

Albany was bankrolling Clifton Park. This was not a problem at the time, but the advice I now give to all business owners looking to open with a partner is put it all down on paper.

Partnership is like a marriage but much worse. There is no make-up sex, or at least there wasn't for me and Caleb.

The arguments started small and slowly grew: whether to allow rebounding on box jumps, how to coach the air squat to new athletes, potentially firing another coach. Resentment was building. Years later, I realized much of this could have been prevented with better communication. At the time, I argued like I was right—and also listened like I was right.

As the years passed, our friendship became increasingly strained. We still hung out, double dated at Chipotle regularly but there was a constant tension.

It came as no surprise to me the day that Caleb approached me and said he wanted to split the business. The negotiations got nasty and ended, as Jerry Seinfeld would say, "a good compromise (where) neither party is happy."

I have no regrets. Our past is what shapes us. Without it, who knows where we would be. I live by the mantra "all for good"—a tattoo my wife and I share on our wrists. Talk about crazy first dates. But I feel badly that it ended the way it did. I know, at some point in my life, we will touch base again when we are both ready.

Lesson 22

Failure is Inevitable

*"Success consists of going from failure to
failure without loss of enthusiasm."*
—WINSTON CHURCHILL

From the moment I took my L1 in Canada, I knew I
wanted to be on the CrossFit Seminar Staff.

I was lucky in that Coach Glassman presented the entire
seminar. Also helping were Nicole Carroll, Dave Castro, Pat
Sherwood and Eva Twardokens. I was starstruck.

I sat in the front row. From the second the seminar
began, I was fully engaged—with the lectures, the workouts
and with the lifelong friends I made that weekend.

I got home very late Sunday evening and immediately
emailed Nicole Carroll to find out how I could become part of
this crew. Turns out they weren't hiring. But, if I held tight a
few months, she said, they would send me more information.
So, I did. I waited for roughly six months. Nothing happened.

Demo'ing the pushup at one of my many L1 internships.

So, I followed up. Nicole said if I came back for a second L1, I could intern. I jumped at the opportunity.

My then-girlfriend and a few Albany CrossFit members decided to take the seminar. We drove to Brooklyn for the first L1 in New York State at CrossFit South Brooklyn.

I wasn't given much information other than "show up at 8 a.m."

The weekend was great. I got to work with Adrian Bozman, Chuck Carswell, Rob Miller, EC Synkowski and a few other veteran Seminar Staff members. At the end of the weekend, I asked if I was now on staff. The response: "Hit us up this week, and we can chat." I was disappointed.

I followed up only to be told, again, that they weren't hiring right now but they would keep me in mind.

Albany CrossFit continued to grow and I opened CrossFit Clifton Park. But I never relinquished my dream to be on Seminar Staff. So, I contacted Dave Castro, co-director of CrossFit's Training Department. I told him that while I was not a Games-level athlete, like most Seminar Staff members at the time, I was knowledgeable, passionate and would do anything it takes. He got me enrolled in the intern process. Again.

As I drove to my internship in Morristown, New Jersey, I was excited but nervous. The process had become more formal. I was sent an itinerary of expectations. I would be interning with Jon Gilson, the founder of Again Faster. He was someone I looked up to. This was referred to as my first internship, even though it was my second. At the end of the weekend, I was told I did great and would be invited back for another seminar to coach the small break-out groups.

I practiced relentlessly. When I wasn't coaching classes at the box, I was reviewing CrossFit's nine foundational movements. I knew them inside and out. Right around the same time, one of my coaches, Austin Malleolo, was also interning for Seminar Staff. He got hired on his second internship. His success emboldened me. I went in to the seminar feeling confident that I'd blow them away.

I headed back to Brooklyn, this time to CrossFit Virtuosity. I'd be under the watchful eye of Dennis Marshall. As I coached the breakout groups on squats and presses, Dennis silently observed. I couldn't tell if I was doing amazing or this was the worst coaching he'd ever seen. He stood there emotionless as I told people to push their knees out and wiggle their toes.

While I coached the deadlift, Dennis stepped in to fix one of the participant's positions. My heart sank. How could I not have seen that? I was ready to run out of the gym screaming, but I did my best to hold it together. It was an exhausting weekend. At the end, when all the participants had said their goodbyes and thanked us for a life-changing experience, Dennis sat me down.

L1 seminar at CrossFit Morristown.

"Jason, you did great. Participants loved you, you get along great with everyone, but you're just not ready to be on Staff."

I was devastated. Dennis assured me there would be more opportunities. I believed him. But I wanted this so badly. The thought of yet another internship was overwhelming.

A few days after I got home, I contacted Dave Castro again. He reiterated that I got good feedback but wasn't ready to be on Staff. I decided I could either let this be the end of my dream or to do something about it. I continued to coach at the boxes, study the movements and take specialty seminars. About a year later, I contacted HQ again to see if I could intern once more.

I was given my next opportunity under Jen Marshall, Dennis's wife. The weekend went great. But I was once again told to come back for another internship. So, I did. I scheduled my next one. It was under Joe DeGain. After another two days of stress and evaluation, I was, once again, told I wasn't ready.

This time, Joe said, "I want you to take six months and refine your coaching skills."

The theme was always the same: Participants love you, you connect with people, but you're not seeing all the faults.

His comments hit me hard. Another six months?

Still, I refused to give up on my dream.

Six months later, I was back. This time I was interning with Mike Giardina. And this time, I felt confident.

147

L1 seminar at CrossFit South Brooklyn.

I had taken the six months to watch as many reps as possible at the box, looking for hip extension, pulling early, knees caving in, anything and everything. I was slowly becoming a ninja coach, like many of my role models on Staff.

At the end of the weekend, it was time for my talk with Mike.

"Jason, we want you on Staff, but you are just not ready."

Here we go again. Mike was vague with his feedback but assured me my dream wasn't dead. He said I should wait to hear from Dave about what to do next. I begged him for more information, but he wouldn't crack. He just kept telling me to sit tight and wait for an email.

Once again, I drove home from New Jersey, feeling bummed out. I thought about what I could have done better. What did I miss? Should I just give up on this?

That week, Dave Castro emailed me to explain I was to be a part of the shadow process. Basically, I would attend three

L1 seminars and simply watch the trainers coach. It was an opportunity to learn more and fill in the gaps of my coaching ability. I jumped at it. My dream wasn't over.

I shadowed three Staff members: Nicole Gordon, Eric O'Connor and Chuck Carswell. Three of the best in the business. As I watched, I could see just how much of a gap there was between me and the cream of the crop.

These were my seventh, eighth and ninth internships, respectively. Mind you, I was responsible for my own travel and hotel accommodations, and I was spending a lot of time away from home. But I was chasing something big, and to me, it was worth it.

Once the shadow process ended, I was signed up to intern at my 10th seminar under Flowmaster Kurtis Bowler, one of the most intimidating men I know. Bowler is a former police officer and owner of the fourth CrossFit affiliate in the world, Rainier CrossFit. Kurtis is stoic. You will not get much emotion out of this man unless you put a large pizza in front of him, then he is all smiles. That first day, I got nothin'. Kurtis simply watched me coaching breakout groups and took notes.

On Saturday night, the Staff went out to enjoy what is known as "International Cheat Night." On this night, CrossFit Seminar Staff members around the world are known to go out to eat gluttonous amounts of food and drink a few cocktails. We enjoyed our Saturday night and when we got back to the hotel, Kurtis and I sat down to review the day.

**Coaching the Medicine Ball Clean at a
L1 Seminar at CrossFit Southside.**

"Jason, I have to be honest with you, I don't think I'm going to hire you."

Gunshot to the face.

He went on to explain. It was all valid feedback. As we ended our meeting, he advised me to, "Come back tomorrow and do your best."

I went up to my room shaking. I was heartbroken. This was my 10th internship. I had been through the shadow program. After this, there were no more opportunities. This was my last shot at becoming a "red shirt."

I didn't sleep that night. I just lay there thinking about the deadlift breakout group I'd coach the next day. It was my last chance. My mind was racing. How would I teach the setup? Would I spot an early arm pull in the sumo deadlift high-pull? Can I get all my participants to open their hip during the medicine-ball clean?

I started Sunday nervous, tired and scared.

The 50 minutes I taught the deadlift breakout group were a blur.

Afterward, Kurtis and I went outside and sat on a park bench across from CrossFit Morristown.

I don't remember much of the conversation other than Kurtis telling me I could fix a "soup sandwich." I wasn't sure what that meant. Then he said he was going to recommend I be hired on Staff. My eyes welled up. He went on to tell me

Coaching or leading an orchestra, I'm not sure.

I had demonstrated my capability that day. I realized I had let go of the judging, the idea of being evaluated, worrying about what he was thinking of me or what I was missing and just coached my ass off.

It's not much different than life: Don't worry about what others are thinking of you; just be you.

When I was just me and coached as I knew I could, that was all he needed to see.

While my time interning on Staff was one of the hardest things I have ever done, it is also an experience I would never trade as it showed me the value of working hard to achieve a dream.

Now, with over six years as a red shirt, it is still something I take immense pride in and continue to work hard on developing myself to be the best example possible.

It is my greatest accomplishment.

Lesson 23

The Dharma of CrossFit

"Never doubt that a small group of thoughtful, committed citizens can change the world; indeed, it's the only thing that ever has."
—Margaret Mead

*E*very Saturday at precisely 8 a.m., CrossFit red shirts around the world gather for what we refer to as the Day 1 meeting.

We review the entire two-day course, including who is presenting each lecture, who will demonstrate movements, how we will organize breakout groups and the rules by which we must abide. Among these rules is one that has always resonated with me:

"The participant experience trumps all."

More recently, I have been pondering what the sentence means to me.

Celebrating with Chuck Carswell at our wedding.

As I've studied this line, I've studied Buddhism and began to notice an overlap.

Buddhism encourages people to follow a spiritual path that will lead them toward the jewels of life: happiness, freedom, enlightenment.

Buddha's path is a set of eight practical guidelines that can simultaneously end suffering and enhance mental strength, as well as our conviction to follow an ethical way of life.

These eight teachings are simple-yet-effective interdependent truths:

1. **Right View:** This first principle teaches the "right way" of the world. We each have our own views influenced by hope, fear and expectation. The more we can ignore these and see situations from an unbiased perspective, the closer we are to the "right view." When meeting new athletes, for example, we need to keep an open mind toward each one and not allow judgment to cloud our view.

2. **Right Intention:** If we can follow the first principle and let go of our judgement, we can behave in a straightforward way. This absence of preconceived ideas will ensure we can see things as they are. This principle will ensure we are acting based on reality and will follow naturally, if we have the right perception. If we refrain from judging others, every action we take has the right intention.

3. **Right Speech:** If our intentions are pure, then we no longer need to worry about our speech. Everything we say will stem naturally from the right intention and happens effortlessly. Although many in society still frown upon cursing, I have found a well-placed F-bomb is often welcomed because I deliver it without malice.

4. **Right Action:** This guideline preaches simplicity. We should be kind and not harm. Right action is all about being honest and respectful. Actions are manifestations of thoughts. With the right view and intention, we begin to make changes in our thoughts. If we do that, right action will automatically follow. As coaches, we meet people from all walks of life and fitness levels. Through our actions, it is our duty to ensure everyone is having fun and feeling comfortable at our gym.

5. **Right Livelihood:** Buddha urges people to be sincere and find passion in whatever they do. This principle emphasizes that livelihood should be earned in a righteous manner and by doing what we like. Most of the stress in the world is created because of people being stuck in jobs they do not like and spending long hours on something they would rather not do. Often, people wish for jobs that pay better or sound better. Right thought and right action will ensure that the right livelihood is chosen. Being an entrepreneur means you're doing what you love for a living. Your goal is to welcome everyone and be an example that they, too, can pursue their dreams.

6. **Right Effort:** If we now see things as they are, have clear intentions and speech, putting in the right effort comes easily. Aggression, jealousy, manipulation are not concerns because with the right livelihood, the right

156

effort follows. People see coaching and assume it's easy. Good coaches show there's an art to the craft and that it takes hundreds and thousands of hours to develop the required skills.

7. **Right Mindfulness**: This guideline urges us to be mindful of every detail of our experiences. Be mindful in the way we speak, work and interact with others. By doing that, we can be happy. With right effort comes a stress-free mind, which allows optimum output in all work we apply it to. Mindfulness while coaching class is preparation. What will you say during the whiteboard brief? How will you warm up athletes? How many spots are available on the pull-up rig for the workout? By bringing mindfulness to all aspects of your job, you can provide the best experience for your customers.

8. **Right Concentration:** This last guideline is about focusing on the present and whatever we are doing at that moment. Right concentration is a natural outcome when the other guidelines are followed. Being present at a seminar is vital—every hour, minute and second. We coaches often say athletes won't remember every cue or their workout scores, but they will remember their interactions with us. Did we ask them about their lives, families and goals? Did we do it while being completely engaged in the conversation? Make their interactions positive.

You don't need to believe in heaven or hell or chant mantras or even meditate to understand these basic Buddhist guidelines. Buddha's aim was simply to show people how to live in harmony with all living creatures. These principles are based on the idea of cause and effect, something often referred to as karma. Good deeds elicit good results.

Over 100,000 participants have gone through the L1 seminar. At the end of every weekend, whether they pass the test or not, the flowmaster gives closing remarks.

Chuck Carswell has said it best: "You are now all ambassadors of CrossFit. We simply ask you to show the same love and respect you were given this weekend to all the people you interact with inside this community and outside."

Lesson 24

Whole-Message Model

"Send out a cheerful, positive greeting, and most of the time you will get back a cheerful, positive greeting. It's also true that if you send out a negative greeting, you will, in most cases, get back a negative greeting."

—Zig Ziglar

As a member of CrossFit Seminar Staff, I've been lucky enough to travel the world teaching the CrossFit methodology. I've met thousands of incredible human beings and impacted their lives. If you haven't taken the CrossFit Level 1 seminar, you should.

Now, the CrossFit Level 2 Certificate Course, while still an incredible experience, is highly stressful.

I took my Level 2 in 2008 at the original CrossFit box in Santa Cruz, California. It was nerve-racking. I had to teach the sumo deadlift high-pull and the medicine-ball clean in front of people like Nicole Carroll, Pat Sherwood, Dave Castro and even Coach Glassman. Give me a second while I go pee my pants. The weekend was incredibly stressful, but I passed, considering I was one of only three that passed that weekend, I was incredibly proud.

Now, years later, I'm on the other side, evaluating Level 2 seminar attendees. I assess and then provide immediate feedback to help them improve. Still, it remains stressful for both parties. These trainers are paying $1,000 to give up a weekend with their families and coach in front of strangers only to receive a list of what they did wrong and how to improve.

I use the whole-message model often, not only when providing feedback at seminars, but in my daily life.

The whole-message model is a simple method for giving either positive or developmental feedback. I have found it particularly useful when I know a difficult conversation is coming. It can be used for positive feedback, as well, making it even more motivational for the recipient. When created with care, and used to start a conversation, it can ease tensions and create a better understanding.

The whole message model looks like this:

- I see.
- I think.
- I feel.
- I want.

Let me break it down for you.

I see.

Sentence starters:

- I saw
- I observed
- I noticed
- I heard

This has to be something black and white.
Examples:

- I see this athlete has a rounded back.
- I see this person's knees are not tracking their toes.
- I see this person is not below parallel.

At home, it might be:

- Honey, I see that there are dishes in the sink.
- Babe, I see the garbage is full and you just piled something else on top.

There is no arguing about it. This is reality.

161

I think.

Sentence starters:

- I thought
- It makes me think
- My perception is

"I think" is often your conclusion or inference based on what you observe. Typically, this includes stating the impact not only on you but on other people.

Examples:

- I think you were so focused on the setup, you missed the lack of hip extension.
- I think that if you had moved to a different angle you would have seen the fault.
- I think you didn't know the points of performance of the push press.

At home, it might be:

- It seems to me you were so busy today you didn't have time to do this.
- It makes me believe this isn't important to you.

I feel.

Sentence starters:

- I am concerned
- I am sad
- I am angry

Feelings are the expressions of your emotions. While the content of a message is extremely important, the emotions expressed—either verbally or nonverbally—often receive primary attention. The emotion you feel is vital to the other person understanding the effect of their behavior.

Examples:

- I am worried your athlete isn't going to be efficient.
- I am concerned they won't learn to send their hips back and down.
- I feel that with better knowledge of this movement, you can spot the fault.

At home, it might be:

- I am saddened by this behavior.
- I feel frustrated that I have to clean up after you.

I want.

Sentence starters:

- In the future
- Next time
- Going forward

"I want" is a clear statement of the results you expect. Wants are exactly what you would like to see changed, implemented, continued or stopped. This needs to be clearly explained so it's likely to be achieved.

Examples:

- I want you to learn the points of performance of the air squat.
- In the future, put your athletes in a circle to give you better angles to see.
- Next time, break down the movement into this progression.

At home, it might be:

- I want you to put the dishes away after you clean them.
- Next time, please take the garbage out when the bin is full.

Using this model is what has allowed me to give feedback but still have participants leaving happy with their heads held high. The reality is that at the end of the seminar, they are the ones who give the most important feedback. They complete a survey that is sent directly to our bosses: the ultimate feedback.

When interacting with others, we should give feedback with the expectation you're going to receive feedback on your feedback.

I get it. That sounds a little crazy. But think about it: feedback on your feedback.

If every time you spoke to someone, you expected them to tell you how well you spoke to them, you would probably change the way you spoke and the words you chose.

It's basically the golden rule: Do unto others as you would have them do unto you.

If I'm using the whole-message model with my wife, it immediately puts her at ease because she understands I'm coming from a good place.

When I first started working L2 seminars, my groups often looked dejected, unhappy and unmotivated.—the exact opposite of what I was looking to do. The big shift involved how I spoke to them. I now begin with feedback on myself: "I know it's strange coaching in front of peers. It's something we do often as Seminar Staff." Or I share how nervous I was

165

at my L2. I'm trying to put them at ease, humanize myself and help them realize I'm only trying to help them develop this skill.

I always tell them, "I have very high expectations of you, and I'm confident you can implement this."

It's a great way to let them know that while I'm going to tell them what they're doing is wrong, it's because I think highly of them. That immediately helps them relax.

Tips to successfully implementing the whole-message model:

1. Prepare your whole message in advance of your conversation. Keep it concise and use the four parts in sequential order. Ideally, this should take less than 30 seconds.

2. For particularly difficult messages, write down what you want to say and practice delivering the message before your conversation.

3. Limit the data in your whole message to no more than three observations, two thoughts, two feelings, and one want.

4. The "I think" portion needs to be about your thoughts— no one else's. Keep it logical and objective—a natural conclusion based on your observations so it can't be argued.

166

5. Don't skip "I feel." At first, many people say "I feel" and then share another thought or conjecture rather than their emotions. Sharing thoughts and feelings separately is the power of the model. It helps the recipient understand the impact of their behavior because you are shifting from the objectivity of observations and thoughts to the revealing of your personal emotions about the situation. This shift from thoughts to feelings, if done well, often deflates any defensiveness.

6. When delivering "I want," keep it objective and focused on future positive behaviors rather than the future omission of negative behaviors.

7. Lastly, if the conversation starts to derail, change tactics and focus simply on active listening. Nothing works better to relax someone else's negative reactions than to listen to them and paraphrase what they say. Active listening is not agreeing. It is communicating to the other person that you have heard him.

Lesson 25

You Never Know What Someone Else Is Going Through

"Be pitiful, for every man is fighting a hard battle."
—Ian Maclaren

At 8 a.m. one Saturday morning, I sat down with the other Seminar Staff members to prepare for the Level 1 seminar that weekend at Reebok CrossFit One in Boston, Massachusetts. We reviewed the standard list: reviewing injuries, participant experience, act professionally, the usual. At the end of the meeting, my good friend and fellow Seminar Staff member Austin Malleolo looked at us and said, "Remember, you never know what someone else is going through."

That statement resonated with me.

Often, we judge people too harshly through the lens of our own prejudices. If someone is rude to us at the grocery store, we don't consider whether there might be an explanation for the way that person is acting.

It reminds me of a story I heard about a man traveling home on the train with his two children. The kids were behaving terribly, yelling and screaming and being a general nuisance to most of the other passengers. Finally, someone approached the father angrily and told him to get control of his kids. The man looked up and apologetically said, "I'm sorry, we just came from their mother's funeral. My mind was elsewhere."

Wow. Makes you take a step back.

A few months after the L1 at Reebok CrossFit One, I was working another seminar. As check-in was under way, a participant arrived who was not pleasant. His name was Rob; he was curt and didn't smile. It's not the typical excited athlete we see who's expecting a life-changing weekend. I took mental note of it and continued checking in registrants.

Once the seminar started, I presented the "What is CrossFit" lecture. It's my favorite lecture as it sets the tone for the weekend with its explanation of constantly varied functional movement performed at high intensity. I weave my own stories into the 40-minute presentation and know the points at which I'll get a good laugh. I've presented the lecture

Hugging it out with Austin Malleolo while
Dave Castro and David Osorio watch.

over 50 times in my career. But Rob didn't smile once. He stared blankly. Truthfully, it messed with my flow as I tried *not* to focus on the one participant who didn't appear to be having fun.

I finished the lecture and prepared myself for my squat-breakout group, Rob was still on my mind. What was wrong with this guy? Of course, he turned up in my breakout group, too. Great.

I coached Rob as I would anyone else. He barely interacted. Instead, he offered blank stares and what appeared to be minimal effort when it came to the cues and corrections I gave him.

I was frustrated.

I left that group mad—mad at myself and mad at Rob. I pride myself on being able to break down walls and make people feel comfortable, but nothing worked with him. After the next lecture, it was our lunch break and I made a beeline to Rob.

I asked one simple question: "Hey Rob, is everything OK?"

His eyes instantly welled up.

"No, my girlfriend dumped me last night, and I'm just a mess over it."

Here I was getting agitated with him and the poor guy had just had his heart broken. Worse yet, she was cheating on him with his friend from the box and he was not sure if he'd ever be able to step foot into that gym again.

I always tell participants I'll give advice on anything but politics and relationships but I broke that rule for Rob. I passed on the usual lunch-time workout with the crew and just chatted with Rob for the full hour. I told him about my many girlfriends. He told me about his. I let him know that everything happens for a reason. The right girl is out there—and every other cliché I could think of. Lo and behold, it worked.

By the end of that hour, he was smiling. He seemed to feel a lot better about his predicament. He was a different person the rest of the weekend: engaging, high-fiving and making new friends.

As Day 2 came to an end and we were saying our goodbyes, Rob approached me to tell me how much it meant that I simply asked, "Is everything OK?" Instead of allowing his situation to ruin his L1, he had the best weekend of his life.

Had I just assumed he was a dick, not only would I have been wrong, but I would have missed an opportunity to cheer up someone and make a new friend.

I'm proud to say Rob met someone at the new CrossFit box he started going to and plans on getting engaged to the love of his life—just like I told him he would.

Maybe I should be giving out more relationship advice?

Lesson 26

Navigate Without a Map

"Life is either a daring adventure, or nothing."
—HELEN KELLER

To say CrossFit has evolved would be a massive understatement.

If you were training CrossFit in 2006, you were "that crazy guy at the gym." The one running from one piece of equipment to another, using the cable crossover for pull-ups, throwing a basketball filled with sand as a makeshift wall ball and jumping on benches rather than boxes. Back then it was like "Fight Club," with the only difference being that everyone talked about it.

These days, you can spot CrossFitters from a mile away: their shoes, their affiliate T-shirt, the Lululemon gear and well-defined trapezius muscles on women. We are not quite mainstream, but we are on the verge.

The same is true of the CrossFit Games. From being broadcast on ESPN and CBS and doling out millions in prize money, the Games have come a long way from Dave Castro's family ranch in Aromas, California.

At the inaugural 2007 Games, organizers created the first event by pulling colored balls out of a hopper. The result: a 1000-meter row followed by 5 rounds of 25 pull-ups and 7 push jerks (135 / 95 lbs).

And the top prize was a whopping $500 cash handed to you directly by Coach Glassman.

Having been open for less than a year I thought it would be a great idea to throw a competition of my own at Albany CrossFit. James Hobart has credited this as being the catalyst behind all other local CrossFit competitions. Truth is I'm sure that would have happened anyway. But I was the first. I reached out to Dave Castro and he gave me the green light. I had never run a competition before. But I had competed in hundreds of wrestling tournaments, so I knew what I liked and what I didn't.

We mimicked the CrossFit Games' programming with a 5K run, CrossFit Total and a hopper event.

The hopper event started with a 1,000-meter row, followed by 5 rounds of

21 sumo deadlift high-pulls (95/65 lbs.), 15 burpees and 9 thrusters (95/65 lbs.). Keep in mind, I didn't have much equipment. In fact, many local affiliates showed up with

**Leading the athlete briefing at the 2009 Regionals
held in the Albany CrossFit parking lot.**

their own. And we didn't have a pull-up rig. We set a time cap of 20 minutes. No one finished. Epic fail. Judging was basically just counting reps with a pencil and paper as the music blasted over a small Bluetooth speaker. Still, everyone had a great time. And we had future CrossFit stars competing, including 2009 Games champion Tanya Wagner, as well as Heather Bergeron, Sarah Scholl, David Osorio and Dennis Marshall.

Because of my event's success—and the ever-growing popularity of the Games—I was brought on to oversee the Games' sectional and regional events in that part of the country. It came with the standard CrossFit HQ advice: "Don't fuck it up."

Event directors were given the flexibility to create their own events. My brain immediately went into overdrive. I was going to have the coolest regional events. I wrote down my ideas, pieced them together and ran them by Dave Castro. During one of these phone calls I remember him bluntly asking, "Why do you hate CrossFit?" He said it jokingly, but his point was taken. I was overthinking everything. Go back and look at some of these events and you can still see aspects of what he was talking about.

I was responsible for every aspect of the event, including equipment, music and judges. It was a huge undertaking.

The first year went off without a hitch and everyone couldn't wait to come back to the Albany CrossFit parking lot in 2010. Still, I made so many mistakes.

For starters, I was so adamant about adhering to the schedule that I ran most heats early, shorting the athletes' valuable warm-up time. During one event, I remember finding Dave Lipson sleeping in his car. I banged on the window to wake him up and yelled at him to get on the floor to compete.

In preparation for 2010, I had a pull-up rig installed to allow for chest-to-bar pull-ups. But we couldn't attach the rig to the pavement. Athletes complained that as they pulled themselves toward the bar, the bar would move away from them.

Volunteers moving our first ever outdoor rig.

In 2011, I took it one step further and commissioned fabricated equipment. Nowadays you can find sleds in many shapes and sizes, but back then they were hard to come by. Luckily, one of my members, Bo, was a welder. He had made a sled for us at Albany CrossFit, and our members loved it. This sled was heavy. Pushing it empty was a challenge in itself, let alone loaded with additional weight. I asked him to make eight for the upcoming regionals and he obliged. The rub was each of these was slightly different. Add to that the fact that our parking lot wasn't exactly even or smooth and you had an event where some lanes were significantly easier than others. My friend Tyler, owner of CrossFit 516, still complains how he was struggling to push an empty sled while women with loaded sleds were flying by him and that cost him his chance to compete at the CrossFit Games.

Here's the point: If you do everything by the book, you can be successful. But if you live your life too much by the book—afraid to take risks, only willing to follow the exact route laid out for you—you'll be limited. Listen to your gut, too. It might show you a shortcut and, every once in a while, you'll discover something new.

(Top) The 2009 North East CrossFit Regionals; (Bottom)
The infamous sled at the 2011 Regionals.

(Top) MC'ing at the 2014 Mid Atlantic Regional; (Bottom) David Osorio and I preparing for the 2012 Regionals at Reebok HQ.

(Top) Rob Orlando celebrating a 3 reps of 300lb
touch and go clean and jerks; (Bottom) volunteers
are the glue that hold together CrossFit events.

Lesson 27

Stay in Your Lane

"I'll either do what I can to make it happen or
deal with the things I have no control over."
—Amy Morin

*E*very year, 40 of the world's best CrossFit trainers gather
to judge the CrossFit Games.

We're sleep deprived, fed way too many peanut M&M's
and asked to judge thousands upon thousands of reps
each within milliseconds of one another. We get slammed
on social media by spectators watching from the comfort
of their own homes—not from a venue packed with tens
of thousands of people and certainly not from the proper
vantage point. It's great. Truly one of the highlights of
my year.

The week begins with a meeting led by Adrian "Boz"
Bozman, Games head judge. We review the announced
events—the rest we find out often times when competitors

Boz most likely telling me to stay in my lane.

do—and we practice nutty drills with our fingers to ensure we're correctly counting double-unders. We're also told in no uncertain terms that we may not speak about these events. At the conclusion of this meeting—and throughout the week—Boz reminds us of two important mantras:

1. Stay in your lane. Misplaced initiative is often worse than doing nothing.
2. Focus on your task at hand. Ignore everything else.

Throughout the week, we meet often and for long hours. People are tired, hungry, agitated. Questions start coming up: Where will the chalk buckets be? Who's changing the weight? What about this? What about that?

Boz often answers swiftly and quietly, "Don't worry about that."

He's right. We don't need to care if an athlete has chalk or who changes the weight on the barbell or whether the competitor can reach the pull-up bar. We are there for one job and one job alone: judge movement.

Imagine if we transferred these principles to our everyday lives.

Inside the box, do we need to care what other peoples' times are? If they hit all their reps? How they're scaling the workout?

Don't get me wrong, I walk into the box every day for class and look at the whiteboard to see what a good time is and what my buddies got so I can try to beat them. But, ultimately, the competition is not with them; it's with me. Am I better than I was yesterday? If I can beat my buddy Vince on the way, that's just gravy.

Outside the box, we focus on what other people have: How much money do they make? What kind of car do they drive? How many Instagram followers do they have?

In the process, we forget what we have.

In his seminal book "The 7 Habits of Highly Effective People," Stephen R. Covey present two circles: the outer circle being your circle of concern and the inner one representing your circle of influence. The point he makes is that we all are concerned with many issues—the economy, global warming, politics, etc. These are all a part of our circle of concern.

How many of these issues can you directly influence?

We all care about the economy, but how can you as an individual impact it? Unless your career involves world finance and you have a direct line to the stock market, chances are this concern does not fall within your circle of influence. Your time would be much better spent on things you can actually control—like how much money you save every pay period or whether you're spending beyond your means. It's like the old adage, "Everybody's talking about the weather, but nobody ever does anything about it."

Spend less time worrying about others and more time figuring out how you can be the best version of yourself. Chances are this doesn't involve comparing yourself to others. It means taking a long, hard look in the mirror and becoming self-aware so you can focus on your priorities.

Lesson 28

The Love You Take is Equal to the Love You Make

"Where there is love there is life."
—Mahatma Gandhi

By 2018, everyone was finding CrossFit. The Games had been on national television, it was featured in news stories and everyone knew someone who was doing it.

In my circle of college friends, I've always been the guy who works out. In school, my buddies would regularly reach out to me when they wanted to put on some muscle. That continued past college, except nowadays they were asking me how to lose their newfound "dad bod." Any time I would see these friends, they would remark how good I looked for 40. Meanwhile, I was often in shock at how heavy

The magic is in the community.

most of them had gotten. When you surround yourself with CrossFitters, you forget what the real world looks like.

Not sure what finally caused my buddy Joe to reach out to me. Did his wife tell him to lose weight? Did he get out of breath playing with his two kids? Did one of my social-media posts hit home? In any case, he sent me a text saying he was ready to try CrossFit.

In school, Joe was one of my regular lifting buddies. While we hit a standard bodybuilding routine back in the day, we'd always focus on compound movements and the big lifts: bench press, deadlift, squat. Joe was my spotter the first time I benched 225 lbs. and yelling in my face the first time I buried a 315-lbs. back squat. But once we graduated, he spent more time in the office than the gym and it was evident by his waist circumference.

In 2007, when someone told me they were ready for CrossFit, I'd go bananas—anxious to create another convert and teach them the ways of fitness. Ten years later, while it still excites me, I had learned that many express interest. Getting them into the box was a different story. Seeing as how I lived in Florida now and Joe was in Long Island, New York, it wasn't as easy as, "meet me there tomorrow."

One thing I should mention about Joe: Even though he's a great guy and super friendly, he's got RBF (resting bitch face). He's not a dick; he just looks like one.

He agreed to hit a few boxes in his hometown to find the one that best suited his needs, class times, traffic patterns, cost, showers, etc.

Here was the text he sent after his first class:

"Dude, WTF. That workout was ridiculous, I thought I could crush it...but I'm the last one done and then all of a sudden everyone is gathered around me like a damn cult cheering me on and yelling at me. I hated it."

My response: "No, that's the box you should join."

I've been to hundreds of boxes. I've seen some really good coaching, and I've seen some really bad coaching. I've seen boxes that were so clean you could eat your dinner off the floor and boxes where I was afraid of catching hepatitis.

But what you can't put a price on, what can't be manufactured, is the culture of the box.

I've coached thousands and thousands of hours. And I say the same thing to my classes every time: As soon as you finish, do your little bacon sizzle, catch your breath, remember your name, and then find someone still working and go cheer them on.

It's what I do.

Your box will only be as successful as your community allows.

Like most things in life, people try to create hacks and shortcuts.

I see affiliates advertising a monthly "bring a friend" Saturday class as their way of building a community. While it helps, that's not how you create an authentic culture.

Culture starts from the top and trickles down—from the owner, to the coaching staff, to each and every member. There is no hack to it.

Next time a class ends, take a look around.

Are people putting their equipment away or cheering on their classmates?

What do you do?

From Day 1 at Albany CrossFit, I made it a point to know more than just every member's name. I knew their jobs, their kids' names, their passions, their goals inside and outside of the box, and a lot ore. It's why over 10 marriages came from the Albany CrossFit community. Because we were a family. We cared about one another, we were in the trenches together.

From Day 1, no class put away equipment until everyone was done. It's what makes one affiliate stand out from another. As CrossFit continues to grow and more and more boxes open, it's not the equipment you buy or the price of your membership, or even how many parking spots you have that will separate you from the other affiliates. It will be the culture you create.

Do people leave your box having had the best hour of their day?

Everything that Joe didn't like is exactly why I knew this was the box for him. But before I explained that to him, I couldn't resist the chance to make fun of my old friend: "It's really easy Joe. If you don't want to be cheered on, don't be last!"

Lesson 29

Define Your Success

*"It is not the style of clothes one wears, neither the
kind of automobile one drives, nor the amount of
money one has in the bank, that counts. These mean
nothing. It is simply service that measures success."*
—George Washington Carver

When I finally sold Albany CrossFit in July 2014 after
months of negotiating, lawyers and contracts, I was ecstatic. At
first. It was more money than I ever imagined having and I had
done the impossible: turned this tiny, dirty gym that started
with nothing more than $500 into a nearly seven-figure sale.

Then I got depressed.

Albany CrossFit was my life, my baby, it was my
everything, and I just gave it away?! How could I? My
financial planner talked some sense into me, but like any
break-up I had a rebound affair. Two months later, I opened
a third box.

Coaching and babysitting at CrossFit Soulshine.

Like a true rebound, she was the exact opposite of my ex. CrossFit Soulshine was shiny and new, and located in the swankiest part of town. We had all the bells and whistles: flat-screen TVs, leather couches, even fancy toilets and squatty potties.

It didn't make me happy.

I eventually left Soulshine and relocated to Florida.

Not owning a box was exhilarating, I was not tied to any geographical location. I could go away whenever I wanted, work seminars every weekend and even found time to start a new company focused on nutrition.

Along the way, I made new friends and even met my wife, Roz, at an L1 seminar.

But I never felt successful. I was always chasing something. I just didn't know what.

It culminated one night in our kitchen as I explained to Roz how I felt like our business wasn't growing fast enough. Roz being the much cooler-headed and rational one in our relationship responded that it was because I equated success to financial gain. As long as I did that, she explained, I'd never be happy.

How did I manage to marry someone so wise *and* so beautiful!?

At 9 a.m. the next day, I found myself in a devastating partner WOD of dumbbell thrusters and double-unders at North Naples CrossFit. I happened to be paired with the owner of the box, a complete freak of nature named Dario. We finished with the fastest time of the day. As I lay in a crumpled heap of my own sweat and DNA, Niki, another member sat down next to me.

She was new, having recently switched from another local affiliate. We had just become friends on Facebook the night before.

Group picture at Albany CrossFit.

With the North Naples CrossFit team, left to right, Matt Torres, Dario Aviles, and Sophia Smith.

"I was stalking you on Facebook," she said. "And I saw what Roz did for your 40th birthday. That was so amazing."

That year, Roz had reached out to dozens of people—almost all of whom I'd met through CrossFit—and asked them to record a short video on how we met and what our friendship meant to them. Roz gave this to me on the night of my 40th birthday. As I watched, my emotions overwhelmed me. I laughed and cried as I watched dozens upon dozens of people joke around, express their love and tell stories of our friendship.

"You're truly rich," Niki's said.

The profundity of her statement hit me hard.

All this time I was so hellbent on defining success through financial gain that I overlooked the ways in which I was already rich: rich in friendship, rich in health, rich in experiences.

I was fulfilled in a manner that no amount of money could eclipse.

Lesson 30

Life is Happening Right Now

"The fear of death follows from the fear of life. A man
who lives fully is prepared to die at any time."
—"A Voice Crying In The Wilderness" by Edward Abbey

When I sold Albany CrossFit, then CrossFit Clifton Park and ultimately my share of CrossFit Soulshine, I felt amazing. I had more money than I ever dreamed of, and I was "retired." I smirk when I say that because anyone who knows me knows I'm far from retired, but now I get to choose what I work on—something referred to as "financial freedom."

It was time to change my life. I had lived in Albany, New York, for 20 years. I moved there in 1996 for college and never left. It was time for a change. The deal was sealed when I hit a huge chunk of snow that ripped off my front bumper during a particularly bad winter night.

"I have enough money," I thought. "I'm moving to Florida!"

I no longer had any attachments to Albany—no businesses to run, no reasons to stick around. I quickly sold my house and gave away just about everything I owned. I wanted to start fresh. I posted on Facebook that I was moving. Most people thought it was a joke. But when April 1st came, I started the 2,000-mile drive down the coast. This was real.

As I was settling into my new surroundings, I was feeling slightly depressed. Now that I no longer owned gyms, I felt that I no longer had an identity. Sure, I coached at some local affiliates, but it wasn't the same. Sure, I got respect for being an L4 coach, but it wasn't the same as being the owner—the man responsible for the decision-making.

I got comfortable with the so-called "Dirty South" L1 Seminar Staff and quickly assimilated into their culture. But something was still off.

For most of my life, the beach represented vacation. I would see it once, maybe twice each year on family vacations. The sun would shine, the sand would stick to you, and I associated it with time away from the real world. Now, living two miles from the beach I had that every day. I made it part of my routine to get to the beach at least one day each week to walk and reflect.

It was on one of these days where my life, once again, changed. I had decided to go for a swim. I had been adding the activity into my routine as an active-recovery day. I was swimming in my usual area off Vanderbilt Beach and had gotten a little farther out than I should have when my right hamstring cramped. At that exact moment, a wave hit me, and I drank what seemed like a gallon of ocean water. I went into full panic mode, flailing around. That only helped me swallow even more salt water.

"What if this is it?" I thought. "Am I going to die? Is this how it ends?"

I focused on each breath and on avoiding panic. Once I chilled the fuck out, I slowly doggy-paddled my way back to the sand, where I collapsed. My eyes welled up. The moment hit me hard. I realized that, just like everyone else, I'm going to die. One day.

I started asking myself more questions: Who am I? What's my legacy? How will the world be different and better because of me?

Instead of focusing on what I no longer was, I remembered what I had created. I remembered the lives I had changed, the friendships I made, the couple that had met and married and had children. I also remembered the person I was before all that.

I sat on the beach for an hour. The longer I sat, the more I reflected. The more I reflected, the lighter I felt. I realized I had been a part of something bigger than me.

The people I met along the way would always look back with fond memories of Albany CrossFit—the PRs, the laughs, the high-fives, the butt slaps. That would never go away, whether I lived in New York or Florida or whether I had taken my last breath that day. This was my legacy. And by being a successful entrepreneur, I helped other entrepreneurs grow: my chiropractor, my yoga studio, my masseuse. I was able to share the wealth.

Confronting my mortality was what I needed.

Yes, we are all going to die. We should come to terms with it. Yes, death is unpleasant, but it's inevitable. Once we become comfortable with it, we can be less restrained and freer to live fully.

With death being the only certainty in life, the only way we can be comfortable with that is understanding we are part of something bigger than ourselves.

"When I was 5 years old, my mother always told me that happiness was the key to life. When I went to school, they asked me what I wanted to be when I grew up. I wrote down 'happy.' They told me I didn't understand the assignment, and I told them they didn't understand life."

That's one of my favorite quotes. It helps us understand that happiness comes from caring about something greater than you—your family, your church, your gym, whatever you decide

As I sat on the beach soaking it all in, an older woman stopped, bent toward me and asked, "Are you OK?"

"Yes," I replied. "I am alive."

Epilogue

This book wouldn't be complete without a final chapter of where my life has gone since selling my third affiliate.

Here I am writing a book about following your "why" and how it led me to own three boxes that I don't own anymore. That doesn't mean I'm no longer living by my "why." It's quite the opposite—I have never felt more connected to it.

My third box, CrossFit Soulshine, was in Saratoga Springs, New York—about 30 miles north of my first box, Albany CrossFit. It was an area I had always thought would make for a thriving affiliate. It was untapped—a college town with a young, hip vibe; a few local coffee spots; an outdoor amphitheater; and a race track that drew throngs of wealthy tourists six weeks out of the year.

When I sold Albany CrossFit, I agreed to a 15-mile non-compete clause, meaning if I were going to open another affiliate it was to be at least 15 miles away. That was never in my plans but when Shye, the owner of The Court Club, added it to our sales agreement, it got me thinking. Would I open another box? I had just sold two. Did I want to open a third? What was I going to do with myself?

Around the same time, a former coach of mine and his wife—whom he met at Albany CrossFit—contacted me to see if I would be interested in opening a box with them in Saratoga Springs. Dave and I weren't friends. I actually didn't like him. He was brash, arrogant and thought he knew everything. But, for some reason, I agreed. I liked the idea of being in business with a partner, not a friend. He was a good coach and his wife, Carmen, was a smart attorney. Together, I believed we could run a successful gym. Plus, they lived up there, so I would only have to commute two times each week, and they would handle almost all daily operations.

We opened Sept. 1, 2014, and were immediately successful. Within a month, we had 40 members. By the end of that year, we were right around 100. I implemented everything I had learned from my previous two boxes, and we were crushing it.

Roz and my first picture together, at her L1 in Miami, Florida.

We ordered the perfect amount of equipment, we had a beautiful website from Day 1 and we were crushing it on social media. A decade of experience had paid off.

On one of my days coaching at the box, I was preparing to leave when I realized we had been pelted with over 3 ft. of snow. The usual 30-minute drive took me over three hours. I had to pull over numerous times on the highway to manually wipe off my windshield because the wipers had frozen. It was on that drive that I decided to move to Florida.

Other than this new affiliate, I had no other attachments to the area. I had my friends, a house and a girlfriend I had been seeing a short time. The allure of warm weather outweighed all of those. I walked in my front door, called my real estate agent and told him to list my house. Then, I called Dave and told him he could buy my stake in the box. Shortly afterward, I called my girlfriend to tell her I was moving. All in the same day. It was that quick.

By April I had all of my remaining possessions loaded in my Toyota Prius, including two dogs, and began the drive to Florida. It's mandatory that all Jews retire to Florida. I was just doing it a bit earlier than most.

CrossFit Seminar Staff tends to work on a regional territorial system. I would now be part of the "Dirty South" crew. I'd be working primarily in Orlando, Tampa, Miami,

Roz and I with the CrossFit 7 mile team.

as well as Georgia with the likes of Chuck Carswell, Todd Occhiuto and Jenni Orr.

It was at a seminar at CrossFit Kingdom in Miami, Florida, where I met the owners of CrossFit 7 Mile, an affiliate on the Cayman Islands. We immediately hit it off, and they invited me to visit the following month to give a nutrition talk.

Two weeks later, I was in Miami again for another L1 seminar. This time, I was responsible for registration. I love checking in participants. It's the first opportunity to meet them and start building relationships. That's when I met her.

It wasn't love at first site for either of us, but we got each other's attention. As I checked in Roz, I noticed she had a Cayman address. I mentioned I'd be down there in a couple of weeks. She recognized me as the box had posted fliers to promote my talk. That's really the extent of it. She recalls me using her as an example in the "What is Fitness?" lecture and coaching her on squat therapy. I don't remember. But as is the case with our relationship now, I just smile and say, "Yes, dear."

A couple of weeks later, I visited CrossFit 7 Mile, hit some workouts, gave my talk—which Roz was at—and left my email and phone number. Turns out that's a good way to give someone your digits. Roz and I talked again while I was there, but nothing noteworthy. She was dating someone, as was I. We said our goodbyes, and it was back to the mainland for me.

Over the next few months, Roz and I would occasionally text. At first it was strictly business. But, as these things go, some flirting got interspersed. At some point, we decided to meet up at the CrossFit Games. I would be there judging, she would be spectating. The Games concluded and we met for breakfast Monday morning before my flight home. We agreed on DK's Donuts. Little did we know how much of an impact those baked treats would have on our relationship.

Breakfast didn't last long enough. I had to catch my flight home, and we both agreed we should do this again. Without hesitation, I invited her to Florida. After all, I told her while boasting of my innate geographical knowledge, "Florida must be on the way between California and Cayman." A month later she visited. Two months after that, we were engaged.

Once again, CrossFit had changed my life.

Since then, we've gotten married, driven around the country in a tiny camper, opened a business and traveled the world. We challenge each other every day. Roz pushes me to be the best version of myself, and I am eternally grateful that she will forever reinforce my "why."

Acknowledgements

This book couldn't have happened without CrossFit and Coach Glassman's methodology. I was truly lost in life before my buddy Chad introduce CrossFit to me and I'm not sure where I'd be without it. I am forever grateful.

First and foremost, thank you to my brilliant and beautiful wife, Roz, who never hesitates to give me her honest opinion about my thoughts and ideas. I knew I was onto something with the concept of this book when I mentioned it to her, saw her reaction and she said, "that's actually a good idea." It's what motivated me to sit down first thing every morning and write.

To all of my members, clients, and participants, past, present, and future that have given me the privilege and honor of coaching them. These lessons come from each and everyone of you and I continue to try and better myself daily in hopes of inspiring all of you. Shout out to my original crew back in 2007, I don't know how you put up with me, thank you for always listening and believing in me.

Thank you James McDermott for always being a sounding board for my ideas and brainstorming. From intern to friend. I am proud of how far you have come.

To the CrossFit Seminar Staff. From the bottom of my heart, thank you. Earning that red shirt is the greatest achievement of my life and I genuinely look forward to every weekend with you.

And finally, to the greater CrossFit community. At this point in my life, I have put in my 10,000 hours and continue to read and study, but you all continue to be my true education. Thank you.

Mom, this is my third book, do you believe I have a real job now?

Thank you so much for reading

BEST HOUR OF THEIR DAY

Please take a moment and leave me
a review on *Amazon*. This is the best
way to help spread the word.

Made in the USA
Monee, IL
24 February 2020